Arthur's
Mystery Envelope

ISBN 979-11-93992-79-1 14740

Longtail Books

For my wonderful editor, Maria Modugno,

who really knows how to polish Arthur's star

Chapter 1

The **cafeteria** at Lakewood Elementary was filled with kids eating lunch. Some of them had brought sandwiches from home. The rest were eating school lunches. Today's choices **feature**d a mystery meat covered in gravy.★

A few teachers **wander**ed between the tables trying to **keep** the noise **under control**.

"Let's keep it down," said Mr. Ratburn. He shook his head. "I don't think anyone's listening."

★**gravy** 그레이비. 고기를 익힐 때 나온 육즙에 밀가루 등을 넣어 만든 소스.

Miss Sweetwater **nod**ded. "Or maybe they just can't hear us," she said.

At one of the middle tables, Arthur and his friends were finishing up.

Arthur was **poking** at his food with a fork. "Even without the gravy," he said, "we'd have no idea where this came from."

"Ready for action, boys?" Francine asked.

"Ready," said Arthur. He **put aside** his **tray**.

"And waiting," said Buster.

They started a game of milk hockey. Francine and Sue Ellen **made up** one team. Arthur and Buster were the other. They used a **crush**ed milk **carton** as a puck,* hitting it **back and forth** the **length** of the table.

Francine **dodge**d left and **flip**ped the carton past Arthur's hand. Buster tried to stop it, but the puck **slid** past him off the table.

★**puck** 퍽. 아이스하키 경기에서 사용하는 작은 원반 모양의 공.

"Goal!" said Muffy. She was the official **scorekeeper**.

Francine smiled. "That didn't take long," she said.

Arthur **flex**ed his hands. "We just take a little while to **warm up**."

"All right," said Sue Ellen. "Let us know when you're nice and **toasty**."

"Maybe we'll need a **substitution**," said Buster. He turned to Binky Barnes. "Do you want a turn?"

"No," said Binky, crushing another carton with his **fist**. He just liked making pucks.

*"**Attention**, please!"*

Miss Tingley, the school **secretary**, was speaking over the **loudspeaker**.

*"Arthur Read, please **report** to **Principal** Haney's office **immediately**."*

A **hush** fell over the room. Everyone was **staring** at Arthur. Buster's mouth was wide

open. Binky's hand had **frozen** in mid-crush.

"Uh-oh!" said Francine.

"**I'll say**," said Muffy.

Sue Ellen just shook her head.

"You're in real trouble now, Arthur," said Buster. Sometimes Mr. Haney **yell**ed at him for running through the halls. But he had been to the *office* only once—for putting **sneezing** powder on Mr. Ratburn's desk.

"Are you all right, Arthur?" Francine asked.

"I-I guess."

"He doesn't look all right," said Sue Ellen. "He looks like one of those **deer** you read about. The ones who stare into the car headlights."

"He's in shock," said Binky. "He**'s** not **used to** visiting the principal's office. I could get there **blindfold**ed with one hand **tie**d behind my back."

"What did you do, Arthur?" asked Francine.

Arthur shook his head. "I don't know. Nothing that I can think of."

Binky **snort**ed. "Don't **bother** trying that **excuse** on Mr. Haney. It never works for me."

Arthur stood up. "Well, I guess I should go."

"Nice knowing you, Arthur," said Francine.

"Good luck," said Buster. "And if you're not planning to finish those potatoes . . ." He pointed to Arthur's **plate**.

Arthur slid over his tray. "**Help yourself**," he said. "I just lost my **appetite**."

Chapter 2

When Arthur got back to the classroom, his friends **rush**ed to his side.

"You **survive**d!" said Buster.

"With no **obvious** signs of **torture**," Binky added. He looked a little **disappoint**ed.

"What happened?" asked Francine.

Arthur **let out** a **sigh**. "Mr. Haney gave me this." He held up a large brown **envelope**. "He said it was for my mom."

"That's it?" asked Muffy. She reached out for a closer look. "What does it say? Is it **seal**ed?"

Francine **grab**bed the envelope. "It's sealed, all right." She held it up to the light. "And too **thick** to read through."

"Give it a shake," said Buster, **cock**ing his ears.

Francine shook the envelope for a moment. It **rustle**d softly. "That doesn't tell us much," she said.

Binky **fold**ed his arms. "Let's just open it."

"I can't," said Arthur. "It's **address**ed to my mother. And look what's **stamp**ed on it: PRIVATE and CONFIDENTIAL."

"That's a bad sign," said Buster. "Good news is never private."

"Besides," said Binky, "you can't start making **excuse**s until you know what kind of trouble you're in."

"Didn't Mr. Haney give you any **clue**s at all?" Francine asked.

"He said it was important," said Arthur,

taking back the envelope. "That was about it."

"If it was good news," said Muffy, "Mr. Haney would have told you. My mother always tells me right away if we've gotten a new **limousine** or if the cook is making a special **dessert** for dinner."

"He didn't say anything like that," Arthur **admit**ted.

"That means it's bad news," said Francine. "The question is, how bad is it?"

This was not a question Arthur wanted to think about.

Binky laughed. "Oooooh! I'll **bet** you lost a library book."

"I don't think Mr. Haney gets **involve**d with **overdue** library books," said Arthur. "Besides, I just returned all mine."

"Oh, no!" said Francine.

"What?" said Muffy.

"Tell us," said Buster.

"Tell me!" said Arthur.

"**Never mind**," said Francine. "It's too **terrible** to think about."

Arthur turned **pale**. "That's why you have to tell me."

"All right," said Francine. "But you **forced** me into it." She **shudder**ed. "What if you didn't pass Mr. Ratburn's **history** test?"

Arthur **frown**ed. The big test had been the week before. It had been a hard one.

"Remember, Arthur? You told me **afterward** that you wrote how the Pilgrims* came to America in 1620."

"Francine, the Pilgrims *did* come to America in 1620."

She looked **surprise**d. "Really?"

Everyone else **nod**ded.

"Well, still . . ." Francine **tap**ped the

★**Pilgrims** 1620년에 신앙의 자유를 위해 메이플라워호를 타고 영국에서 미국으로 건너가 매사추세츠주 플리머스에 정착한 청교도.

envelope. "The **proof** is right here. And if you failed that test, you might fail the whole year. You know what that means: summer school."

Arthur sat down in his chair and thought about his **fate**. Summer school. Perhaps the two most **dread**ed words in the English language.

*He saw himself **chain**ed to the wall of a dark **dungeon**. Outside the **bar**red window, he could hear his friends playing. He looked out through the bars. Buster and the Brain were setting up a tent for camping. Muffy and Prunella were Rollerblading.*

*Arthur looked around his **cell**. He was alone—with only some thick, **dusty** books for **company**. Then the **guard**, Mr. Ratburn, walked in. He was **slurp**ing ice cream from a cone. A few drops fell on the stones, just beyond Arthur's reach.*

"**Snap out of it**, Arthur!" said Buster.

Arthur looked at his friend **blank**ly.

PRIVATE
CONFIDENTIAL

"You know what they say," Buster went on. "Those who don't learn their history are **doom**ed to repeat it."

Arthur sighed. History or not, he felt doomed **for sure**.

Chapter 3

Arthur could have taken the **envelope** straight home after school. But he didn't.

"Mr. Haney didn't say anything about *when* you should **deliver** the envelope," the Brain had told him. "Under international law, you have the **right** to make a plan."

They were sitting in a **booth** at the Sugar Bowl. Buster and Francine were there, too. Prunella and Muffy were **seat**ed behind them.

Arthur had bought some candy, but he wasn't eating it. He was just moving it around in front of him. The candy was **shaped** in a

rectangle with a big question mark inside it.

The Brain was **staring** hard at Arthur's envelope. "If only I could use X-ray **vision** . . . ," he said.

Buster **grab**bed the envelope from him. "We have to **take action**! I don't want to **spend** all summer doing fun **stuff** without you." He pushed the envelope toward the **edge** of the table. "Hey, what if you **accidenta**lly lost it?"

He **shove**d the envelope onto the floor.

"It could **end up** in the **trash**. Or a **shredder**. Then **bulldoze**d into a **landfill**. Only the **seagull**s would read it there. And we don't have to worry what they think."

"That's true," said Arthur.

Prunella picked up the envelope.

"Don't listen to him, Arthur. He doesn't **look ahead**. You need to think of something that won't be **blam**ed on you in the end." She **paused**. "Maybe you could hide it in the

laundry basket—and it could get *washed*." She picked up the envelope and held it carefully as if it were wet and **drip**ping. "She won't be able to read it, but you won't be blamed."

"Laundry," said Arthur. "Interesting."

"Not interesting," said Muffy. "**Risky**. You need to get it as far away from your house as possible. Buy it a first-class ticket to Alaska* or Timbuktu.*"

"I don't have that kind of money," said Arthur.

He looked at the clock. It was time to go home.

Everyone went outside.

Francine was still **frown**ing. "There must be some way out of this," she said.

The Brain looked down at the storm **drain**.

★**Alaska** 알래스카. 미국 북서부에 위치한 주(州).

✴**Timbuktu** 팀북투. 아프리카 말리(Mali)의 북부에 위치한 도시로, 아주 멀리 떨어진 곳을 일컬을 때 흔히 사용된다.

THE SUGAR BOWL

"You could drop it in here," he said. "The **current** would carry it into Bear Lake and from there to the Otter River. Once it was in the **harbor**, it would be carried out to sea—maybe even to Europe. When it **eventually** washed up on **shore**, it's possible a mother might find it. But she probably wouldn't understand English, so you'd be safe."

"Europe is far away," said Arthur.

Francine **pluck**ed the envelope from the Brain's hand. "Don't do it, Arthur," she said. "If you try to lose it, you'll be in double trouble—for losing it *and* for whatever you did **in the first place**."

She handed the envelope back to him.

"The whole thing doesn't seem **fair**," said Arthur. "I didn't do anything! I'll just have to give the envelope to my mother and see what happens."

He had hoped saying that would make

him feel better. It didn't.

"That's a **last resort**," said the Brain. "But, of course, the choice is yours."

Chapter 4

"Hello!" Arthur called out softly.

No one was in the kitchen except his dog, Pal. Arthur knew his mother was home, though. Her car was in the **driveway**.

"But she could be busy," he told Pal. "In fact, I'm sure of it. She could be working or helping D.W. or taking care of baby Kate. I don't want to **disturb** her."

Pal **bark**ed.

"Are you hungry?" said Arthur.

Pal **wag**ged his tail.

Arthur put down his **backpack** on the

counter. One corner of Mr. Haney's **envelope** was **stick**ing **out** of the **flap**. Then he began **rinsing** out Pal's food dish.

"Mr. Haney told me the envelope was for Mom," Arthur explained to Pal. "But he didn't say what was in it."

Pal barked.

"No," said Arthur, "I can't eat the envelope."

Pal barked again.

"No, I can't **bury** it in the **backyard**, either."

He put the empty dish on the floor. Pal **whine**d with **disappoint**ment.

"All my friends think the news must be bad," Arthur went on.

Pal continued to whine.

"Francine thinks I failed Mr. Ratburn's **history** test. She says I'll have to go to summer school." Arthur **made a face**.

Pal jumped up and down at his side.

Arthur **fetch**ed the dog food from the

pantry. "Maybe I'll just leave it out and not say anything. Mr. Haney said I should bring it home to her. He didn't say I **actually** had to *give* it to her. Maybe she won't even **notice** it."

Arthur **laid** the dish on the table, then opened his backpack. He **remove**d the envelope carefully and put it on the table.

"What's that?"

Arthur **whirl**ed around to find his sister D.W. standing in the **doorway**.

"What's what?"

D.W. pointed. "The envelope, **silly.**"

"Nothing!" he **shout**ed. He **lean**ed on the table. "It's just a **dumb** old envelope. People could walk by this envelope for weeks and not even notice it. And even if they did notice it, they wouldn't **bother** to open a **boring** envelope like this."

"That's a lot of nothing," said D.W. "You sure are acting **weird**."

"I'm not acting weird," said Arthur. He **straighten**ed up and **fold**ed his arms. "I'm worried. I mean, I'm not worried. I'm hurried. That's it. Hurried. Third grade is very busy."

D.W. climbed onto a chair and **stare**d into Arthur's eyes. "You don't **fool** me," she said. "I know *worry* when I see it."

Arthur **blink**ed. "You do?"

D.W. **nod**ded. "Yup.★ You get **wrinkle**s."

"I do?"

She nodded. "I'm not **surprise**d. You could worry about lots of things. Like maybe someday you'll be too old for birthday presents. Or maybe you think there really is a boogeyman,✳ and he's just waiting for the first night you **forget** to check under your bed."

★ **Yup** 'yes'의 구어체. 응, 그럼.
✳ **boogeyman** 못된 아이를 데려간다는 귀신.

27

CONFIDENTIAL
PRIVATE

Arthur **sigh**ed. "Those are **regular** worries. Everyday worries. I can **handle** those."

D.W. gave him a careful look. "You mean there's *more?* **Come on, spill the beans.**"

"All right, all right!" said Arthur. "The **principal** just gave me this envelope for Mom. That's all. Now leave me alone!"

But D.W. wasn't finished yet. She took a look at the envelope. "What are these words?" she asked.

"Which words?"

"These big words on the front."

"PRIVATE and CONFIDENTIAL."

D.W. **frown**ed. "I know PRIVATE. What does CON-FI-DEN-TEE-UL mean?"

Arthur sighed. "That only Mom can look at it."

D.W.'s eyes opened wide. She got down from the chair and **skip**ped toward the hall, singing,

For once Arthur didn't **argue** with her. He knew she was right.

The good news was that D.W. suddenly stopped singing. The bad news was that she stopped because she had **bump**ed into her mother.

"Slow down, sweetie. We can't **afford** to put a **traffic light** in here."

Mrs. Read gave D.W. a quick kiss. Her hands were full of papers.

"What a day! If I had two heads and four hands, I'd still be behind."

Mrs. Read was an **accountant**. She always got a little **frazzled** at **tax** time.

"Mom, Arthur's acting a little **weird**. He brought home a—"

"Hey!" said Arthur. "That's none of your—"

"**Hush**, Arthur!" said his mother. "Not now, D.W. I've got a few calls to make."

She put her papers down on the **counter**.

"Arthur, what is this?"

Arthur **cringe**d. "That?"

"Yes, that." She pointed to the **envelope** and Pal's dish beside it. "On the table."

"The table? Here? In the kitchen?"

His mother **fold**ed her arms. "Yes, the kitchen table. Since when does Pal eat there?"

Arthur **let out** a deep **breath**.

"He doesn't."

"Then why did you leave his dish on the table?" She put it down on the floor. "**Honestly**, Arthur, I **expect** you to be more careful."

PAL
PRIVATE
CONFIDENTIAL

While Arthur **fidget**ed, Mrs. Read picked up the phone and **dial**ed a number. She left a message with the **secretary**.

"That's my third try this afternoon. That man is just impossible to reach." She **glance**d at Arthur. "Is everything all right? You look a little **pale**."

"Of course," said Arthur. "I was just thinking about, um . . . setting the table for dinner." He pulled out some forks and knives from a **drawer** and began placing them in front of each chair.

"Mail call!*" said Mr. Read, arriving with a **bundle** of letters. He dropped them on top of Arthur's envelope.

"How is everyone today?"

"Dear, you have **whip**ped cream behind your ear."

★ **mail call** 군대에서 대원들의 우편물을 배포할 때 하는 말.

"Really? I thought I had cleaned it all up."
He **scrape**d the cream off with his finger. "I
was **experiment**ing with a new **dessert**."

Mr. Read was very busy with his **catering**
business.★

"I hope no one was hurt," said Mrs. Read.

Mr. Read **sigh**ed. "Only the **piecrust** didn't
survive."

The phone rang.

"I'll get it," said Mrs. Read. She picked up
the mail and the envelope as she answered
the phone. "Hello? Oh, hi, Leah."

She started to look through the mail.

One letter went into the **wastebasket**.

"No, no, I'm not disappointed you called. I
was just expecting to hear from Herb."

She **put** a **bill aside** for later.

★**catering business** 음식 출장 서비스 사업. 파티나 각종 행사를 위해 음식 및
테이블, 의자 등을 고객의 가정이나 특정 장소로 출장 서비스하는 사업.

"I needed some **paperwork** from him."

She **flip**ped through a **magazine**.

"Yes, I know. It's all **due** Monday."

Arthur watched his mother with an **increasing** sense of **doom**. He **edge**d his way to the door. His mother had reached Mr. Haney's envelope.

Suddenly the water on the **stove** began **bubbling** over.

"Oh, I've got to run," said Mrs. Read. "Talk to you later, Leah." She **hung up** the phone and dropped the envelope on the edge of the counter. She turned back to the stove.

The envelope **teeter**ed for a moment—and then fell into the wastebasket.

Arthur **slump**ed with **relief**. He was **innocent**. He hadn't put the envelope in the **trash**. Some other hand had **guide**d it there. It was **fate**. It was **destiny**. It was meant to be.

Chapter 6

Dinner was hard to **swallow**. How could Arthur **concentrate** on eating? Every time he looked up, he saw the **envelope peek**ing at him from the **wastebasket**.

Even the fact that they were having hamburgers and potato puffs* hadn't **cheer**ed him up. His partly eaten hamburger sat on the **edge** of his **plate** like a **crescent** moon. Usually he **pile**d the potato puffs into a castle wall and then lined up the green **bean**s like

---

★ **potato puff** 감자튀김. 감자를 으깨어 일정 모양을 만든 후 기름에 튀겨낸 음식.

alligators in the **moat**. But tonight he had only **stamp**ed the puffs and beans down with his fork. They looked like little **shred**ded carpets.

"Are you trying to save **wear and tear** on your teeth, Arthur?" asked his mother.

Arthur looked **confuse**d.

She pointed to his plate. "All that **mash**ing. You still have to eat them, you know. We don't want to waste food."

Arthur took a small **bite**.

His father **help**ed **himself** to some salad. "You're **awful**ly quiet tonight, Arthur," he said.

Arthur **squirm**ed in his chair. "We worked hard in school today." He looked at his father. "When you were in school, were tests important?"

"Oh, yes. We didn't have all the different projects you kids have today. Sometimes a single test could be half our whole grade."

"That much?"

His father smiled. "**Definite**ly. I wouldn't say you kids have it easy, but you do have more choices."

"Most important," said Mrs. Read, "we want you to do your best."

"I always do my best," said D.W., who was **swap**ping potato puffs with Kate. "It's all part of my plan."

"What plan is that, sweetie?" asked her mother.

"Her plan for world **domination**," said Arthur.

"Arrrthur!" said his father.

"Sorry." Arthur changed the subject. "Do you think every part of school is important? I mean, don't some parts **matter** more than others?"

Mr. Read shook his head. "That's hard to say. At your age I never planned on having a **catering** business. And even though my business is food, I still need to know math for planning and how to write for **advertising**."

"What about, um, history?" said Arthur. "That wouldn't matter so much, would it?"

"History's important, too," said his father. "I might want to study old **recipe**s or **create** a **meal** with some **historical theme**."

"I see," said Arthur, wishing he didn't. "It **makes sense** to learn about everything," said his mother. "You can't tell when it might come in **handy** later on." She looked down the table. "Arthur, pass me the potato puffs, please."

Arthur picked up the **bowl**.

D.W. smiled. "Arthur, isn't there anything else you'd like to give Mom **while you're at it**?"

Arthur just **barely** kept himself from kicking D.W. under the table. "Just my

thanks," he said, "for making this great dinner."

He forked up some mashed puffs and beans and filled his mouth.

His mother looked at him. "Thank you, Arthur—I think."

She might have said more, but the phone rang. She jumped up to get it.

Saved by the bell, thought Arthur—at least **for now.**

After dinner, Arthur went to his room to do his homework.

*Think of a word that **rhyme**s **with** rope *and* hope.*

"Arrghhh!" said Arthur.

He **switch**ed quickly to math. The first problem **involve**d cutting a **rectangle** in half.

"I wish I could cut that **envelope** in half," said Arthur.

Another question was about a **mailbag** filled with letters. There was no **mention** of the *E* word, but that was all Arthur could think about.

He began **doodling** on the **edge** of his
paper. He started with a big rectangle, an
enormous rectangle, the largest rectangle in
the world.

*But was it only a rectangle? No, it was a giant
envelope, and it was* ***chasing*** *Arthur down a hill.
It* ***tumble****d* ***end over end****. Arthur could* ***barely***
keep ahead of it.

*"Don't run," the envelope was saying. "I know
you'll* ***fit*** *nicely inside me. And don't worry. I will
never let you out."*

"No, thank you," said Arthur. "I'll get
flatten*ed." He ran faster.*

"That's not my fault," said the envelope,
huffing *and* ***puffing****. "I'm just not in very good
shape."*

Arthur **rub**bed his eyes. He needed a break.

He took a **peek** in Kate's room. She was
already asleep.

"Babies are lucky," he **mutter**ed. "They don't have to worry about envelopes. Or **history** tests. Or summer school. They only have to look **cute** and fill their **diaper**s."

Kate turned in her sleep, and her **blanket slip**ped off her.

Arthur put it back. "The good old days," he **sigh**ed.

His mother was sitting in her office. She was **chew**ing on a pencil and **hum**ming while she worked. Arthur **tiptoe**d past the door. He found his father and D.W. watching *The Karaoke** *Kitten*s show on TV.

The kittens were wearing **straw** hats and dancing **in a line** while they sang.

"Those kittens are crazy," said D.W. "Watch carefully now. This is the best part."

"How do you know?" asked her father.

★ **karaoke** 노래방. 본문에서는 '고양이 노래방 쇼'라는 TV프로그램 이름으로 나왔다.

Arthur sat down. "She's seen this episode eighty-four times," he explained.

"And it just gets better and better," said D.W. She shook her head **in time** with the music.

Her father hummed along. "Not every kitten can dance like that," he **point**ed **out**. "It takes a lot of **practice**."

A **commercial** came on.

*"Is the stress of everyday life **get**ting **you** down?"*

Arthur **nod**ded.

"Do you feel like you're no longer in control?"

Arthur nodded again.

*"The **pound**ing, the pounding. It just won't stop."*

Arthur **cradle**d his head in his arms.

*"For the chance to feel like your old self again, try Painfree or Painfree Plus. **Headache relief** is just minutes away."*

Arthur stood up. If only he could take a **pill** to **get rid of** his problem. But things were not that easy.

"You really look tired, Arthur," said his father.

"I am," Arthur **admit**ted.

"Sshhhh!" said D.W. "The kittens are going to sing '**Fur** Ball.' I love that song."

Arthur didn't stay to hear it. With a quiet "Good night," he went up to bed.

As Arthur got ready for bed, he found himself looking at his **pillow**. He had never **notice**d before how much it looked like a **stuff**ed **envelope**.

While **brush**ing his teeth, Arthur brought his face right up to the mirror. His teeth lined up in little **square row**s.

Almost like envelopes, he thought.

Everywhere he looked—the **wallpaper**, the **carpeting**, the pattern on his **blanket**—he saw envelopes. They came in every **shape** and size.

"I **have** envelopes **on the brain**," he decided. "What I need is a good night's sleep."

Arthur climbed into bed and pulled up the covers.

"Are you still **awake**, Arthur?"

D.W. was standing in the **doorway**.

"No. I'm **sound asleep**. You're a bad dream. Go away."

"If you're sound asleep, how can you tell me to go away?"

Arthur sat up. "What do you want?"

"I want to know about the trouble you're in."

"There's no trouble, D.W."

She was not **convince**d. "What was in that mysterious envelope?"

"I don't know," Arthur said **honestly**.

"Mom didn't **mention** it to you?"

"No, she didn't."

"Oh." D.W. was **disappoint**ed. "Don't

worry. I'm sure you'll get in trouble for something else."

"Thanks, D.W. That makes me feel much better."

"Anytime," said D.W., and went back to her room.

Arthur **stare**d at the **ceiling**. **Strictly** speaking, he had told D.W. the truth. His mother *hadn't* mentioned to him what was inside the envelope. Of course, that was only because she hadn't *seen* it yet. The envelope was still sitting in the **wastebasket**.

Why can't it just stay there? thought Arthur.

He closed his eyes for what seemed like only a second.

His eyes opened.

*Arthur heard some paper **rustling**. What was making that sound? He got out of bed and listened.*

*The sound was coming from **downstairs**.*

Arthur followed the noise into the kitchen. The wastebasket was shaking—as if something was **bouncing** around inside it. Arthur looked down. Mr. Haney's envelope was growing bigger right before his eyes! The wastebasket could no longer hold it.

Arthur pulled the envelope free and ran upstairs. The envelope was **flap**ping in his arms. It was getting too big to carry. Arthur **drag**ged it along the floor to the bathroom. He **hoist**ed it into the **tub** and drew the shower curtain.

The curtain shook and **trembl**ed.

Arthur screamed—and **fled** downstairs into his mother's arms.

"What's going on?" she asked.

Arthur **grab**bed her arm and pulled.

"We have to get out of the house, Mom. It's getting too big!"

As they stepped outside, one corner of the envelope **wriggl**ed through a window. Another

PRIVATE
CONFIDENTIAL

popped out of the **chimney**.

"What's going on?" asked his mother.

"It's the envelope," **yell**ed Arthur. "Don't open it! It could be something **horrible**!"

At that moment the roof flew off the house. The top of the envelope rose up, and the flap opened.

D.W. popped out.

"You **trick**ed me, Arthur," she said. "You haven't even told Mom yet."

"Noooooo!" cried Arthur.

Chapter 9

Arthur woke up. His hands were **cross**ed in front of his face.

"I can't go on this way," he **mutter**ed. "Even summer school would be better than this."

He walked **downstairs**. His father was still watching TV. It was some kind of cooking show.

"Parsley, sage, rosemary, and thyme may make for a good song title, but don't use them together as **seasoning**s."*

★ **parsley, sage, rosemary, thyme** 향신료로 쓰는 허브들. 파슬리, 세이지, 로즈메리, 타임.

"It might be **worth** trying," Mr. Read said to himself. "Maybe in a soup . . ."

Arthur kept going. His feet felt like **lead**, and his legs seemed to be moving in slow motion.

The **envelope** was still in the **wastebasket**. Arthur picked it out.

He walked over to the dining room, where his mother had her work area.

The light was still on.

Arthur took a deep **breath**. "It's going to keep **bother**ing me until I **get this over with**."

He entered the dining room.

"Do you have a second, Mom?"

His mother put down her pen. "For you, two seconds.* But why are you up so late?"

★ **two seconds** 잠깐 시간이 있냐고 물을 때 "Do you have a second?"라고 하는 데, 글자 그대로 보면 "(잠깐 내어줄) 1초(a second)를 가지고 있냐"는 뜻이다. 여기서 는 이 말을 장난스럽게 받아서 "너한테는 1초뿐만이 아니라 2초(two seconds)도 내어 줄 수 있다"고 답하고 있다.

TAX.

Arthur took a deep breath. "That's what I need to talk to you about. I **was supposed to** do something **right away** when I got home. But I was worried I might be in trouble, so I didn't do it, and now I'm afraid you're going to get mad—"

"Slow down, Arthur! What's going on? You can tell me. I won't get mad."

"Promise?"

She **nod**ded.

Arthur handed her the envelope. She **slit** it open and **glance**d inside.

"Ah! Here it is!" She **frown**ed. "Arthur, I've been waiting for this all night."

Arthur looked down at the floor. "You said you wouldn't get mad."

"Yes, yes, I did." His mother took a deep breath. "Well, I'm not mad **exact**ly. *Frustrated* would be a better word. I'm very frustrated. I've been trying to reach Herb for hours. I need this information."

"But this is from Mr. Haney."

"Herb is his first name.*"

She glanced through the papers.

"Um, Mom?"

"Hmmmm. . . . Yes, Arthur?"

"What's in there?"

His mother looked up. **Tax document**s. I'm doing his tax return.*"

"**Nothing to do with** me?"

"Not unless you want to help Mr. Haney pay his taxes!"

Arthur laughed. "Good-bye, summer school," he **murmur**ed.

Mrs. Read put down her papers for a moment. "Now I think I understand," she said. "But Arthur, even if this was about you,

---

★ **first name** 이름. 지위나 관직에는 보통 성(last name)만 붙여 말하기 때문에, 아서는 엄마가 연락하려고 하는 Herb씨가 Harney 교장 선생님인지 모르고 있었다.

✳ **tax return** 소득 신고. 납세 의무자가 세법에 의하여 소득 신고서를 제출하는 행위.

we would need to know."

"What if it was something bad?"

His mother **sigh**ed. "**Putting off** bad news doesn't make it get any better. And sometimes it makes it worse. Besides, Dad and I can't help you with a problem if we don't know you have one."

Arthur nodded. "I guess that's true."

"Well, we can talk more in the morning. Now back to bed, honey. It's late."

She gave him a kiss.

All that worrying for nothing, thought Arthur. He had **tortured** himself all afternoon and evening for no good reason.

"**Cheer** up, Arthur," said his mother. "You're not disappointed, I hope. Because if you really want to be in trouble, I'm sure I could **arrange**—"

"Good night, Mom!" Arthur said **hurried**ly, and **bolt**ed for the door.

Chapter **10**

It was too late for Arthur to call his friends, but he could imagine their **reaction**s.

"You're still alive?" Francine would say. **"Way to go!"**

Buster would be **please**d, too. "Now we'll be together all summer! If you get in any trouble then, I'll be right there beside you."

"Rats,*" Binky would say. "You got **off the hook** again? I can't believe it."

As Arthur was about to head up the stairs,

★ **rats** (속어) 젠장, 이런.

he saw D.W. waiting for him.

"So, tell me what happened!" she said. "Are you **ground**ed for a year? Off to **jail**? Can I have your room?"

"Back to bed, you two!" their mother called out.

"I'm just getting a drink," said D.W. She **stare**d at Arthur. "I'm waiting. . . ."

Arthur **shrug**ged. "Sorry to **disappoint** you, D.W., but there's nothing to tell. I don't know where you get these crazy ideas."

"Crazy ideas? Where do I get them?" She stopped to think. "Let me see. I wasn't the one **frozen** in **terror**. Or **jumpy** as a **frog**."

"Frozen? Jumpy?" Arthur's eyes opened wide. "What an **imagination**!"

"**Come on**," said D.W. "Tell me. Are you moving into the **garage**? Is Pal moving there with you? Are we—"

"Enough questions," said Arthur. "I'm not

telling you anything."

"You're not?"

Arthur smiled. "D.W., this is one mystery you'll have to solve on your own."

She **made a face** at him, but Arthur didn't care. He felt better at last.

아서의
미스터리한 봉투

아서의 미스터리한 봉투
(Arthur's Mystery Envelope)

1판 1쇄   2013년 7월   8일
2판 1쇄   2025년 7월 28일

지은이   Marc Brown
기획   김승규
책임편집   차소향 김보경
콘텐츠제작및감수   롱테일 교육 연구소
저작권   홍하늘
마케팅   두잉글 사업본부

펴낸이   이수영
펴낸곳   롱테일북스
출판등록   제2015-000191호
주소   04033 서울특별시 마포구 양화로 113, 3층(서교동, 순흥빌딩)
전자메일   help@ltinc.net

이 도서는 대한민국에서 제작되었습니다.

ISBN 979-11-93992-79-1 14740

CONTENTS

초보 영어 학습자라면 꼭 한번 읽어 봐야 할, 아서 챕터북 시리즈!

『아서 챕터북(Arthur Chapter Book)』 시리즈는 레이크우드(Lakewood) 초등학교에 다니는 주인공 아서(Arthur)가 일상에서 벌이는 다양한 에피소드를 담고 있습니다. 저자 마크 브라운(Marc Brown)이 미국 초등학생들을 위해 쓴 이 시리즈는, 누구나 공감할 만한 재미있는 스토리 덕분에 출간된 지 30년이 넘은 지금까지도 남녀노소 모두에게 큰 사랑을 받고 있습니다. 아서가 주인공으로 등장하는 이야기는 리더스북과 챕터북 등 다양한 형태로 출판되었으며, 미국에서만 누적 판매 부수 7천만 부를 돌파하고 TV 애니메이션으로 제작되는 등 높은 인기를 구가하고 있습니다.

특히 『아서 챕터북』 시리즈는 한국에서 초급 영어 학습자를 위한 최적의 원서로 큰 사랑을 받고 있기도 합니다. 많은 영어 교육 전문가들과 영어 학습법 도서에서 『아서 챕터북』 시리즈를 추천 도서로 소개하고 있으며, '엄마표 · 아빠표 영어'를 진행하는 부모님들에게도 반드시 거쳐 가야 하는 영어원시로 큰 지지를 얻고 있습니다.

번역과 단어장이 포함된 워크북, 그리고 오디오북까지 담긴 풀 패키지!

이 책은 영어원서 『아서 챕터북』 시리즈에, 탁월한 학습 효과를 거둘 수 있도록 다양한 콘텐츠를 덧붙인 책입니다.

- **영어원서**: 본문에 나온 어려운 어휘에 볼드 처리가 되어 있어 단어를 더욱 분명하게 인지할 수 있고, 문맥에 따른 자연스러운 암기 효과를 얻을 수 있습니다.
- **단어장**: 원서에 볼드 처리된 어휘의 의미가 완벽하게 정리되어 있어 사전 없이 원서를 수월하게 읽을 수 있으며, 반복해서 등장하는 단어에 '복습' 표기를 하여 자연스럽게 복습을 돕도록 구성했습니다.
- **번역**: 영문과 비교할 수 있도록 직역에 가까운 번역을 담았습니다. 원서 읽기에 익숙하지 않은 초보 학습자도 어려움 없이 내용을 파악할 수 있습니다.
- **퀴즈**: 챕터별로 내용을 확인하는 이해력 점검 퀴즈가 들어 있습니다.
- **오디오북**: 미국 현지에서 판매 중인 빠른 속도의 오디오북(분당 약 145단어)과 국내에서 녹음된 따라 읽기용 오디오북(분당 약 110단어)을 기본으로 포함하고 있어, 듣기 훈련은 물론 소리 내어 읽기에까지 폭넓게 활용할 수 있습니다.

- 미국 원어민 기준: 유치원 ~ 초등학교 저학년
- 한국 학습자 기준: 초등학교 저학년 ~ 중학생
- 영어원서 완독 경험이 없는 초보 영어 학습자 (토익 기준 450~750점대)
- 도서 분량: 약 5,200단어
- 비슷한 수준의 다른 챕터북: Flat Stanley,★ The Zack Files,★ Tales from the Odyssey,★ Junie B. Jones,★ Magic Tree House, Marvin Redpost

   ★「롱테일 에디션」으로 출간된 도서

『아서 챕터북』 이렇게 읽어 보세요!

- **단어 암기는 이렇게!** 처음 리딩을 시작하기 전, 오늘 읽을 챕터에 나오는 단어들을 눈으로 쭉 훑어봅니다. 모르는 단어는 좀 더 주의 깊게 보되, 손으로 쓰면서 완벽하게 암기할 필요는 없습니다. 본문을 읽으면서 이 단어를 다시 만나게 되는데, 그 과정에서 단어의 쓰임새와 어감을 자연스럽게 익히게 됩니다. 이렇게 책을 읽은 후에 단어를 다시 한번 복습하세요. 복습할 때는 중요하다고 생각하는 단어들을 손으로 쓰면서 꼼꼼하게 외우는 것도 좋습니다. 이런 방식으로 책을 읽으면 많은 단어를 빠르고 부담 없이 익힐 수 있습니다.

- **리딩할 때는 리딩에만 집중하자!** 원서를 읽는 중간중간 모르는 단어가 나온다고 워크북을 바로 펼쳐 보거나, 곧바로 번역을 찾아보는 것은 크게 도움이 되지 않습니다. 모르는 단어나 이해되지 않는 문장들은 따로 가볍게 표시만 해 두고, 전체적인 맥락을 파악하며 속도감 있게 읽어 나가세요. 리딩을 할 때는 속도에 대한 긴장감을 잃지 않으면서 리딩에만 집중하는 것이 좋습니다. 모르는 단어와 문장은 리딩을 마친 후에 한꺼번에 정리하는 '리뷰' 시간을 통해 점검하는 시간을 가지면 됩니다. 리뷰를 할 때는 번역은 물론 단어장과 사전도 꼼꼼하게 확인하면서 어떤 이유에서 이해가 되지 않았는지 생각해 봅니다.

- **번역 활용은 이렇게!** 이해가 가지 않는 문장은 번역을 통해서 그 의미를 파악할 수 있습니다. 하지만 한국어와 영어는 정확히 1:1 대응이 되지 않기 때문에 번역을 활용하는 데에도 지혜가 필요합니다. 의역이 된 부분까지 억지로 의미

를 대응해서 이해하려고 하기보다, 어떻게 그런 의미가 만들어진 것인지 추측하면서 번역은 참고 자료로 활용하는 것이 좋습니다.

- **듣기 훈련은 이렇게!** 리스닝 실력을 향상시키고 싶다면 오디오북을 적극적으로 활용해 보세요. 처음에는 오디오북을 틀어 놓고 눈으로 해당 내용을 따라 읽으면서 훈련을 하고, 이것이 익숙해지면 오디오북만 틀어 놓고 '귀를 통해' 책을 읽어 보세요. 눈으로 읽지 않은 책이라도 귀를 통해 이해할 수 있을 정도가 되면, 이후에 영어 듣기로 어려움을 겪는 일은 거의 없을 것입니다.

- **소리 내어 읽고 녹음하자!** 이 책은 특히 소리 내어 읽기(voice reading)에 최적화된 문장 길이와 구조를 가지고 있습니다. 오디오북 기본 구성에 포함된 '따라 읽기용' 오디오북을 활용해 소리 내어 읽기 훈련을 시작해 보세요! 내가 읽은 것을 녹음하고 들어보는 과정을 통해 자연스럽게 어휘와 표현을 복습하고, 의식적·무의식적으로 발음을 교정하게 됩니다. 이렇게 영어로 소리를 만들어 본 경험은 이후 탄탄한 스피킹 실력의 밑거름이 될 것입니다.

- **2~3번 반복해서 읽자!** 영어 초보자라면 처음부터 완벽하게 이해하려고 하는 것보다는 2~3회 반복해서 읽을 것을 추천합니다. 처음 원서를 읽을 때는 생소한 단어들과 스토리 때문에 내용 파악에 급급할 수밖에 없습니다. 하지만 일단 내용을 파악한 후에 다시 읽으면 문장 구조나 어휘의 활용에 더 집중하게 되고, 원서를 더 깊이 있게 읽을 수 있습니다. 그 과정에서 리딩 속도에 탄력이 붙고 리딩 실력 또한 더 확고히 다지게 됩니다.

- **'시리즈'로 꾸준히 읽자!** 한 작가의 책을 시리즈로 읽는 것 또한 영어 실력 향상에 큰 도움이 됩니다. 같은 등장인물이 다시 나오기 때문에 내용 파악이 더 수월할 뿐 아니라, 작가가 사용하는 어휘와 표현들도 반복되기 때문에 탁월한 복습 효과까지 얻을 수 있습니다. 롱테일북스의 『아서 챕터북』 시리즈는 현재 10권, 총 50,000단어 분량이 출간되어 있습니다. 시리즈를 꾸준히 읽다 보면 영어 실력이 자연스럽게 향상될 것입니다.

원서 본문 구성

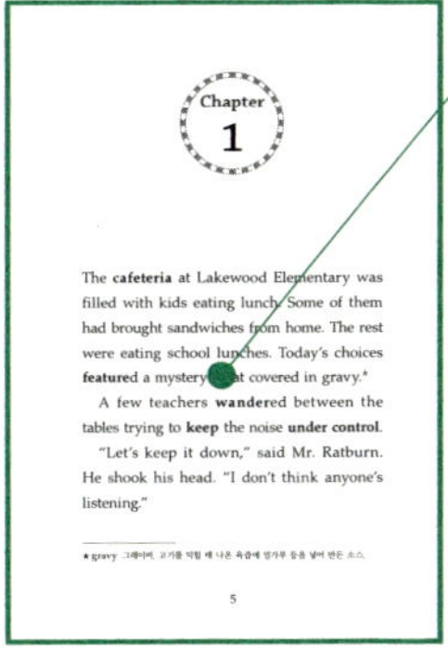

내용이 담긴 원서 본문입니다.

원어민이 읽는 일반 원서와 같은 텍스트지만, 암기해야 할 중요 어휘들은 볼드체로 표시되어 있습니다. 이 어휘들은 지금 들고 계신 워크북에 챕터별로 정리되어 있습니다.

학습 심리학 연구 결과에 따르면, 한 단어씩 따로 외우는 단어 암기는 거의 효과가 없다고 합니다. 단어를 제대로 외우기 위해서는 문맥(context) 속에서 단어를 암기해야 하며, 한 단어당 문맥 속에서 15번 이상 마주칠 때 완벽하게 암기할 수 있다고 합니다.

이 책의 본문에서는 중요 어휘를 볼드체로 강조하여, 문맥 속의 단어들을 더 확실히 인지(word cognition in context)하도록 돕고 있습니다. 또한 대부분의 중요 단어들은 다른 챕터에서도 반복해서 등장하기 때문에 이 책을 읽는 것만으로도 자연스럽게 어휘력을 향상시킬 수 있습니다.

본문 하단에는 내용 이해를 돕기 위한 '각주'가 첨가되어 있습니다. 각주는 굳이 암기할 필요는 없지만, 알아 두면 도움이 될 만한 정보를 설명하고 있습니다. 각주를 참고하면 스토리를 더 깊이 있게 이해할 수 있어 원서를 읽는 재미가 배가됩니다.

워크북(Workbook) 구성

Check Your Reading Speed

해당 챕터의 단어 수가 기록되어 있어, 리딩 속도를 측정할 수 있습니다. 특히 리딩 속도를 중시하는 독자들이 유용하게 사용할 수 있습니다.

Build Your Vocabulary

본문에 볼드 표시되어 있는 단어들이 정리되어 있습니다. 리딩 전·후에 반복해서 보면 원서를 더욱 쉽게 읽을 수 있고, 어휘력도 빠르게 향상될 것입니다.

단어는 〈스펠링 – 빈도 – 발음기호 – 품사 – 한글 뜻 – 영문 뜻〉 순서로 표기되어 있으며 빈도 표시(★)가 많을수록 필수 어휘입니다. 반복해서 등장하는 단어는 빈도 대신 '복습'으로 표기되어 있습니다. 품사는 아래와 같이 표기했습니다.

n. 명사 | **a.** 형용사 | **ad.** 부사 | **v.** 동사

conj. 접속사 | **prep.** 전치사 | **int.** 감탄사 | **idiom** 숙어 및 관용구

Comprehension Quiz

간단한 퀴즈를 통해 읽은 내용에 대한 이해력을 점검해 볼 수 있습니다.

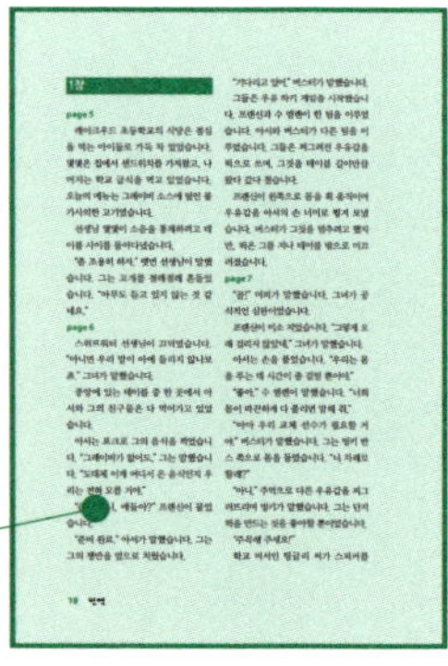

한국어 번역

영문과 비교할 수 있도록 최대한 직역에 가까운 번역을 담았습니다.

오디오북 구성

이 책에는 '듣기 훈련'과 '소리 내어 읽기 훈련'을 위한 2가지 종류의 오디오북이
기본으로 포함되어 있습니다.

- **듣기 훈련용 오디오북**: 분당 145단어 속도 (미국 현지에서 판매 중인 오디오북)
- **따라 읽기용 오디오북**: 분당 110단어 속도 (소리 내어 읽기 훈련용 오디오북)

QR 코드를 인식하여 따라 읽기용 & 듣기 훈련용 두 가지 오디오북을 들어
보세요! 더불어 롱테일북스 홈페이지 (www.longtailbooks.co.kr)에서도
오디오북 MP3 파일을 다운로드 받을 수 있습니다.

Chapter 1

1. **What was featured in the school lunch menu at Lakewood Elementary?**

    A. Ham and turkey sandwiches

    B. Mystery meat covered with gravy

    C. Mashed potatoes covered with gravy

    D. Mystery spaghetti covered with sauce

2. **What game did Arthur and his friends play at lunch?**

    A. Milk hockey

    B. Milk soccer

    C. Milk basketball

    D. Milk football

3. **What message came over the loudspeaker?**

  A. Buster's mom was waiting for him in the principal's office.

  B. Arthur and his friends should stop playing games at lunch.

  C. Arthur should come to the principal's office immediately.

  D. Buster should not put sneezing powder on Mr. Ratburn's desk.

4. **What did Buster think about the news?**

  A. He thought that Arthur was going to get something good.

  B. He thought that Arthur was leaving the school.

  C. He thought that Arthur was going home early.

  D. He thought that Arthur was in trouble.

5. **Why did Arthur give his lunch to Buster?**

  A. Arthur would eat lunch later.

  B. Arthur had lost his appetite.

  C. Arthur lost the game at lunch.

  D. Buster had forgotten his lunch at home.

Check Your Reading Speed

1분에 몇 단어를 읽는지 리딩 속도를 측정해보세요.

$$\frac{509 \ words}{reading \ time \ (\quad) \ sec} \times 60 = (\qquad) \ WPM$$

Build Your Vocabulary

⋆ **cafeteria** [kǽfətíəriə] n. 셀프 서비스식 식당, 구내식당
A cafeteria is a restaurant where you choose your food from a counter and take it to your table after paying for it.

⁑ **feature** [fíːʧər] v. 특징을 이루다, 특별히 포함하다; n. 특색, 특징, 특성; 특집
When something such as a film or exhibition features a particular person or thing, they are an important part of it.

⋆ **wander** [wándər] v. 돌아다니다, 걸어다니다; 방황하다, 헤매다
If you wander in a place, you walk around there in a casual way, often without intending to go in any particular direction.

keep something under control idiom ~을 제어하다, 억누르다
If you keep something under control, it is being dealt with successfully and is unlikely to cause any more harm.

⁑ **nod** [nad] v. (고개를) 끄덕이다, 끄덕여 나타내다; n. (고개를) 끄덕임
If you nod, you move your head downward and upward to show agreement, understanding, or approval.

⋆ **poke** [pouk] v. (손가락 등으로) 쿡 찌르다; n. 찌르기, 쑤시기
If you poke someone or something, you quickly push them with your finger or with a sharp object.

put aside idiom ~을 한쪽으로 치우다
If you put something aside, you place it to one side.

★ **tray** [trei] n. 쟁반

A tray is a flat piece of wood, plastic, or metal, which usually has raised edges and which is used for carrying things, especially food and drinks.

make up idiom ~을 이루다, 형성하다

If you make up something, you put several different things together.

⁂ **crush** [krʌʃ] v. 잔뜩 구겨지다; 으스러뜨리다; 밀어 넣다

To crush something means to press it very hard so that its shape is destroyed or so that it breaks into pieces.

★ **carton** [kɑːrtn] n. (음식이나 음료를 담는) 곽, 통; 상자

A carton is a plastic or cardboard container in which food or drink is sold.

back and forth idiom 앞뒤로, 좌우로

If someone moves back and forth, they repeatedly move in one direction and then in the opposite direction.

⁂ **length** [leŋkθ] n. 길이; (무엇이 계속되는 긴) 시간

The length of something is the amount that it measures from one end to the other along the longest side.

★ **dodge** [dadʒ] v. (재빨리) 피하다, 날쌔게 비키다, 몸을 홱 피하다; n. 발뺌

If you dodge something, you avoid it by quickly moving aside or out of reach so that it cannot hit or reach you.

★ **flip** [flip] v. 홱 뒤집(히)다, 휙 젖히다; (책장을) 휙휙 넘기다; n. 톡 던지기; 공중제비

If you flip something, especially a coin, you use your thumb to make it turn over and over, as it goes through the air.

★ **slide** [slaid] v. (slid-slid) 미끄러지듯 움직이다; 미끄러지(게 하)다; n. 미끄러지기

When something slides somewhere or when you slide it there, it moves there smoothly over or against something.

scorekeeper [skɔ́ːrkìːpər] n. (경기의) 득점 기록원

A scorekeeper is an official who writes down the score of a game or competition as it is being played.

flex [fleks] v. (준비 운동으로) 몸을 풀다
If you flex your muscles or parts of your body, you bend, move, or stretch them for a short time in order to exercise them.

warm up idiom (스포츠나 활동 전에) 몸을 천천히 풀다, 준비 운동을 하다
If you warm up for an event such as a race, you prepare yourself for it by doing exercises or by practicing just before it starts.

toasty [tóusti] a. 훈훈한, 따끈따끈한
If something is toasty, it is comfortably warm.

* **substitute** [sʌ́bstətjùːt] v. 대신하다, 대치[교체]되다 (substitution n. 교체 선수)
If you substitute one thing for another, or if one thing substitutes for another, it takes the place or performs the function of the other thing.

* **fist** [fist] n. (쥔) 주먹
Your hand is referred to as your fist when you have bent your fingers In toward the palm in order to hit someone.

* **attention** [əténʃən] n. 주의, 관심; 배려
If you give someone or something your attention, you look at it, listen to it, or think about it carefully.

* **secretary** [sékrətèri] n. 비서; 총무, 서기
A secretary is a person who is employed to do office work, such as typing letters, answering phone calls, and arranging meetings.

loudspeaker [láudspìːkər] n. 확성기, 스피커
A loudspeaker is a piece of equipment, for example part of a radio, through which sound comes out.

* **report** [ripɔ́ːrt] v. 출두하다; 알리다, 발표하다, 전하다; n. 보도
If you report to a person or place, you go to that person or place and say that you are ready to start work or say that you are present.

* **principal** [prínsəpəl] n. 교장, 학장, 총장; a. 주요한, 주된
The principal of a school is the person in charge of the school.

✱ **immediately** [imíːdiətli] ad. 곧바로, 즉시
If something happens immediately, it happens without any delay.

✭ **hush** [hʌʃ] n. 침묵, 고요; v. ~을 조용히 시키다; int. 쉿, 조용히 해
You say there is a hush in a place when everything is quiet and peaceful, or suddenly becomes quiet.

✭ **stare** [stɛər] v. 응시하다, 뚫어지게 보다
If you stare at someone or something, you look at them for a long time.

✱ **freeze** [friːz] v. (froze–frozen) (두려움 등으로 몸이) 얼어붙다; 얼다, 얼리다
If someone who is moving freezes, they suddenly stop and become completely still and quiet.

I'll say idiom (맞장구치며) 그럼, 맞아, 내 말이 그 말이야
I'll say is used to show that you agree very strongly with what has been said.

✭ **yell** [jel] v. 소리치다, 고함치다; n. 고함소리, 부르짖음
If you yell, you shout loudly, usually because you are excited, angry, or in pain.

✭ **sneeze** [sniːz] v. 재채기하다; n. 재채기
When you sneeze, you suddenly take in your breath and then blow it down your nose noisily without being able to stop yourself, for example because you have a cold.

✭ **deer** [diər] n. 사슴
A deer is a large wild animal that eats grass and leaves. A male deer usually has large, branching horns.

be used to ~ idiom ~하는 데 익숙하다
If you are used to something, you are familiar with it because you have done it or experienced it many times before.

blindfold [bláindfòuld] v. (눈가리개로) 눈을 가리다; n. 눈가리개
If you blindfold someone, you tie a blindfold over their eyes.

tie [tai] v. 묶다, 매다; 속박하다, 구속하다; n. 넥타이, 끈
If you tie two things together or tie them, you fasten them together with a knot.

snort [snɔ:rt] v. 코웃음을 치다, 콧방귀를 뀌다; n. 코웃음, 콧방귀
When people or animals snort, they breathe air noisily out through their noses. People sometimes snort in order to express disapproval or amusement.

bother [báðər] v. 신경 쓰다, 애를 쓰다; 신경 쓰이게 하다, 괴롭히다; n. 성가심
If you do not bother to do something or if you do not bother with it, you do not do it, consider it, or use it because you think it is unnecessary or because you are too lazy.

excuse [ikskjú:z] n. 변명, 이유; v. (무례나 작은 실수 등을) 용서하다
An excuse is a reason which you give in order to explain why something has been done or has not been done, or in order to avoid doing something.

plate [pleit] n. (둥그런) 접시, 그릇
A plate is a round or oval flat dish that is used to hold food.

help oneself idiom 마음대로 집어먹다, 자유로이 먹다
If someone tells you to help yourself, they are telling you politely to serve yourself anything you want or to take anything you want.

appetite [ǽpətàit] n. 식욕
Your appetite is your desire to eat.

Chapter 2

1. What did Arthur receive from Mr. Haney?

A. He received a report card for his parents.

B. He received a certificate for sports.

C. He received an envelope for his father.

D. He received an envelope for his mother.

2. Why did Arthur not open what he had received?

A. He wanted to show his best friend first.

B. He was not interested in the letter at all.

C. It was addressed to only his mother.

D. He did not have a letter opener.

3. **Why did Arthur's friends think that it contained bad news?**

   A. Mr. Haney had given Arthur a red envelope.

   B. Mr. Haney had not told Arthur it was good news.

   C. Mr. Haney had told Arthur to forget about it.

   D. Mr. Haney only had bad news for students.

4. **What did Francine think had happened to Arthur?**

   A. She thought that Arthur had failed a history test.

   B. She thought that Arthur had failed a science test.

   C. She thought that Arthur had failed an English test.

   D. She thought that Arthur had failed a math test.

5. **What did Arthur imagine happening to him when he thought of summer school?**

   A. He imagined himself studying diligently and earning high grades in school.

   B. He imagined himself chained to a wall in a dungeon while his friends played outside.

   C. He imagined himself camping outside with his friends on a sunny day.

   D. He imagined himself eating ice cream and reading books with his friends.

1분에 몇 단어를 읽는지 리딩 속도를 측정해보세요.

$$\frac{590 \text{ words}}{\text{reading time (} \qquad \text{) sec}} \times 60 = (\qquad) \text{ WPM}$$

Build Your Vocabulary

⁑ rush [rʌʃ] v. 돌진하다, 급히 움직이다, 서두르다
If you rush somewhere, you go there quickly.

⁑ survive [sərváiv] v. 살아남다, 생존하다
If a person or living thing survives in a dangerous situation such as an accident or an illness, they do not die.

⁑ obvious [ábviəs] a. 명백한, 분명한
If something is obvious, it is easy to see or understand.

⁎ torture [tɔ́ːrʧər] n. 고문; v. 고문하다
If you say that something is torture or a torture, you mean that it causes you great mental or physical suffering.

⁑ disappoint [dìsəpɔ́int] v. 실망시키다, 낙담시키다 (disappointed a. 실망한, 좌절된)
If things or people disappoint you, they are not as good as you had hoped, or do not do what you hoped they would do.

let out idiom (울음소리·신음소리 등을) 내다
If you let out a cry or a sigh, you make a sound.

⁎ sigh [sai] n. 한숨, 탄식; v. 한숨 쉬다
A sigh is a deep breath of expressing feelings such as disappointment, tiredness, or pleasure.

* **envelope** [énvəlòup] n. 봉투
An envelope is the rectangular paper cover in which you send a letter to someone through the post.

* **seal** [si:l] v. (봉투 등을) 봉인하다; 밀폐하다; n. 직인, 도장
When you seal an envelope, you close it by folding part of it over and sticking it down, so that it cannot be opened without being torn.

* **grab** [græb] v. 부여잡다, 움켜쥐다; n. 부여잡기
If you grab something, you take it or pick it up suddenly and roughly.

* **thick** [θik] a. 두꺼운, 두툼한, (부피가) 굵은
Something that is thick has a large distance between its two opposite sides.

* **cock** [kak] v. (귀·꽁지를) 쫑긋 세우다, 위로 치올리다; n. 수탉; 마개
If you cock a part of your body in a particular direction, you lift it or point it in that direction.

* **rustle** [rʌsl] v. 바스락거리다; n. 바스락거리는 소리
If things such as paper or leaves rustle, or if you rustle them, they move about and make a soft, dry sound.

* **fold** [fould] v. (손·팔·다리를) 끼다, 포개다; 접다, 접어 포개다
If you fold your arms or hands, you bring them together and cross or link them, for example over your chest.

* **address** [ədrés] v. (~ 앞으로 우편물을) 보내다, 주소를 쓰다; 연설하다; n. 주소
If a letter, envelope, or parcel is addressed to you, your name and address have been written on it.

* **stamp** [stæmp] v. (도장·스탬프 등을) 찍다; (발을) 구르다; n. 우표; 도장
If you stamp a mark or word on an object, you press the mark or word onto the object using a stamp or other device.

* **private** [práivət] a. 사적인, 개인적인
Your private things belong only to you, or may only be used by you.

confidential [kànfədénʃəl] a. 비밀의, 기밀의; 은밀한
Information that is confidential is meant to be kept secret or private.

excuse [ikskjúːz] n. 변명, 이유; v. (무례나 작은 실수 등을) 용서하다
An excuse is a reason which you give in order to explain why something
has been done or has not been done, or in order to avoid doing
something.

clue [kluː] n. 단서, 실마리
A clue is a sign or some information which helps you to find the answer
to a problem.

limousine [líməzìːn] n. 리무진(대형 승용차)
A limousine is a large and very comfortable car.

dessert [dizə́ːrt] n. 디저트, 후식
Dessert is something sweet, such as fruit or a pudding, that you eat at
the end of a meal.

admit [ædmít] v. 인정하다
If you admit that something bad, unpleasant, or embarrassing is true,
you agree, often unwillingly, that it is true.

bet [bet] v. 틀림없이 ~이다, 확신하다; 걸다, 내기하다; n. 내기, 건 돈
You use expressions such as 'I bet', 'I'll bet', and 'you can bet' to indicate
that you are sure something is true.

involve [inválv] v. (상황·사건·활동이 사람을) 관련시키다; 포함하다
If you say that someone involves themselves in something, you mean
that they take part in it, often in a way that is unnecessary or unwanted.

overdue [òuvərdjúː] a. (지불·반납 등의) 기한이 지난
An overdue library book has not been returned to the library, even
though the date on which it should have been returned has passed.

never mind idiom (중요하지 않으니까) 신경 쓰지 마, 괜찮아
You use never mind to tell someone that they do not need to do
something or worry about something, because it is not important or
because you will do it yourself.

terrible [térəbl] a. 끔찍한; 지독한, 심한; 무서운

If something is terrible, it is very bad or of very poor quality.

pale [peil] a. 창백한, 핼쑥한; (색깔이) 엷은

If someone looks pale, their face looks a lighter color than usual, usually because they are ill, frightened, or shocked.

force [fɔːrs] v. (~을 하도록) 강요하다, 억지로 시키다; n. 힘, 물리력, 폭력

If someone forces you to do something, they make you do it even though you do not want to, for example by threatening you.

shudder [ʃʌ́dəːr] v. (공포·추위 등으로) 몸을 떨다, 몸서리치다, 전율하다

If you shudder, you shake with fear, horror, or disgust, or because you are cold.

history [hístəri] n. 역사(학)

History is a subject studied in schools, colleges, and universities that deals with events that have happened in the past.

frown [fraun] v. 얼굴[눈살]을 찌푸리다; n. 찡그림, 찌푸림

When someone frowns, their eyebrows become drawn together, because they are annoyed or puzzled.

afterward [ǽftərwərd] ad. 나중에, 그 후에

If you do something or if something happens afterward, you do it or it happens after a particular event or time that has already been mentioned.

surprise [sərpráiz] v. 놀라게 하다, 경악하게 하다 (surprised a. 매우 놀란)

If you surprise someone, you give them, tell them, or do something they are not expecting.

nod [nad] v. (고개를) 끄덕이다, 끄덕여 나타내다; n. (고개를) 끄덕임

If you nod, you move your head downward and upward to show agreement, understanding, or approval.

tap [tæp] ① v. (가볍게) 톡톡 두드리다 ② n. 수도꼭지

If you tap something, you hit it with a quick light blow or a series of quick light blows.

‡ **proof** [pru:f] n. 증거(물), 증명(서)
Proof is a fact, argument, or piece of evidence which shows that something is definitely true or definitely exists.

⁎ **fate** [feit] n. 운명, 숙명
Fate is a power that some people believe controls and decides everything that happens, in a way that cannot be prevented or changed.

⁎ **dread** [dred] v. (~을) 몹시 무서워하다; (안 좋은 일이 생길까 봐) 두려워하다; n. 두려움
(dreaded a. 두려운, 무서운)
If you dread something which may happen, you feel very anxious and unhappy about it because you think it will be unpleasant or upsetting.

‡ **chain** [ʧein] v. 사슬로 매다, 속박하다; n. 쇠사슬; 연쇄, 일련
If a person or thing is chained to something, they are fastened to it with a chain.

dungeon [dʌ́ndʒən] n. 지하 감옥
A dungeon is a dark underground prison in a castle.

‡ **bar** [ba:r] v. 빗장을 지르다, 판자를 붙여 막다; n. 막대기 (모양의 것)
If you bar a door, you place something in front of it or a piece of wood or metal across it in order to prevent it from being opened.

‡ **cell** [sel] n. (교도소의) 독방; 세포
A cell is a small room in which a prisoner is locked.

⁎ **dusty** [dʌ́sti] a. 먼지투성이의, 먼지 많은
If a room, house, or object is dusty, it is covered with very small pieces of dirt.

‡‡ **company** [kʌ́mpəni] n. 함께 있음; 회사; (함께 일하거나 공연하는) 단체
Company is having another person or other people with you, usually when this is pleasant or stops you feeling lonely.

‡ **guard** [ga:rd] n. 경비 요원, 보초; v. 지키다, 보호하다, 경비를 보다
A guard is a specially organized group of people, such as soldiers or policemen, who protect or watch someone or something.

slurp [sləːrp] v. (무엇을 마시면서) 후루룩 소리를 내다, 후루룩 마시다

If you slurp a liquid, you drink it noisily.

snap out of it idiom (침울해 하지 말고) 기운을 내다

If you say 'snap out of it' to someone, you mean they should try to stop feeling unhappy or depressed.

⋆ **snap** [snæp] v. 홱 움직이다; 손가락을 튕기다; 딱[툭] (하고) 부러뜨리다; 사진을 찍다

If you snap something into a particular position, or if it snaps into that position, it moves quickly into that position, with a sharp sound.

⋆ **blank** [blæŋk] a. 멍한, 무표정한; 빈; n. 빈칸, 여백 (blankly ad. 멍하니, 우두커니)

If you look blank, your face shows no feeling, understanding, or interest.

doom [duːm] v. 불행한 운명[결말]을 맞게 하다; n. (피할 수 없는) 비운
(doomed a. 운이 다한, 불운한)

If something is doomed to happen, or if you are doomed to a particular state, something unpleasant is certain to happen, and you can do nothing to prevent it.

for sure idiom (의심할 여지없이) 확실히, 틀림없이

If you say that something is for sure or that you know it for sure, you mean that it is definitely true.

Chapter 3

1. **According to the Brain, what did Arthur have the right to do under international law?**

   A. Arthur had the right to make a plan.

   B. Arthur had the right to return the envelope.

   C. Arthur had the right to ignore the envelope.

   D. Arthur had the right to open the envelope.

2. **What did Buster suggest doing with the envelope?**

   A. He suggested hiding it in a book at the library.

   B. He suggested mailing it at a post office.

   C. He suggested accidentally losing it.

   D. He suggested keeping it in his backpack.

3. **Why did Prunella suggest putting it in the laundry?**

   A. Arthur's mother would have a clean letter which would smell nice.

   B. Arthur's mother would not be able to read it, but would not blame Arthur.

   C. Arthur's mother would find and read it quickly, but would not blame Arthur.

   D. Arthur's mother would be shocked and would go to Mr. Haney.

4. **What did Arthur think of Muffy's suggestion of flying the letter far away?**

   A. He did not like airplanes.

   B. He did not have much money.

   C. He did not want anyone else to read it.

   D. He did not know much about Alaska or Timbuktu.

5. **What did Arthur say he would do in the end?**

   A. He could give the envelope to his mother and see what happened.

   B. He could give the envelope to his pet dog, Pal, and see what happened.

   C. He could give the envelope to his father instead of his mother.

   D. He could simply throw the letter away and forget all about it.

1분에 몇 단어를 읽는지 리딩 속도를 측정해보세요.

$$\frac{519 \text{ words}}{\text{reading time ( ) sec}} \times 60 = (\qquad) \text{ WPM}$$

Build Your Vocabulary

envelope [énvəlòup] n. 봉투
An envelope is the rectangular paper cover in which you send a letter to someone through the post.

deliver [dilívər] v. 배달하다, 넘겨주다; (약속 등을) 이행하다
If you deliver something somewhere, you take it there.

right [rait] n. (법적·도덕적) 권리, 권한; 오른쪽, 우측; a. 옳은, 올바른
Your rights are what you are morally or legally entitled to do or to have.

booth [buːθ] n. (식당의) 칸막이된 자리; (칸막이를 한) 작은 공간, 부스
A booth in a restaurant or café consists of a table with long fixed seats on two or sometimes three sides of it.

seat [siːt] v. 앉히다, 착석시키다; n. (앉을 수 있는) 자리, 좌석
If you seat yourself somewhere, you sit down.

shape [ʃeip] v. (어떤) 모양[형태]으로 만들다; n. 모양, 형태
If you shape an object, you give it a particular appearance, which is round, square, curved, or fat.

rectangle [réktæŋgl] n. 직사각형
A rectangle is a four-sided shape whose corners are all ninety degree angles. Each side of a rectangle is the same length as the one opposite to it.

stare [stɛər] v. 응시하다, 뚫어지게 보다
If you stare at someone or something, you look at them for a long time.

vision [víʒən] n. 시력, 눈; 시야
Your vision is your ability to see clearly with your eyes.

grab [græb] v. 부여잡다, 움켜쥐다; n. 부여잡기
If you grab something, you take it or pick it up suddenly and roughly.

take action idiom ~에 대해 조치를 취하다, 행동에 옮기다
If you take action, you start doing something.

spend [spend] v. (시간을) 보내다, 지내다; (돈·자원을) 쓰다, 소비하다
If you spend time or energy doing something, you use your time or effort doing it.

stuff [stʌf] n. 것(들), 물건, 물질; v. 채워 넣다, 채우다
You can use stuff to refer to things such as a substance, a collection of things, events, or ideas, or the contents of something in a general way without mentioning the thing itself by name.

edge [edʒ] n. 끝, 가장자리, 모서리; v. 조금씩[살살] 움직이다, 이동시키다
The edge of something is the place or line where it stops, or the part of it that is furthest from the middle.

accidental [æ̀ksədéntl] a. 우연한; 부수적인 (accidentally ad. 우연히)
An accidental event happens by chance or as the result of an accident, and is not deliberately intended.

shove [ʃʌv] v. 아무렇게나 놓다; (거칠게) 밀치다, 떠밀다
If you shove something somewhere, you push it there quickly and carelessly.

end up idiom 마침내는 (~으로) 되다, 결국 ~로 끝나다
If you end up doing something or end up in a particular state, you do that thing or get into that state even though you did not originally intend to.

* **trash** [træʃ] n. 쓰레기; v. 부수다, 엉망으로 만들다
Trash consists of unwanted things or waste material such as used paper, empty containers and bottles, and waste food.

shredder [ʃrédər] n. (서류를 폐기 처리하는) 파쇄기
A shredder is a machine for shredding things such as documents or parts of bushes that have been cut off.

bulldoze [búldòuz] v. 불도저로 밀다, 부수다
If people bulldoze something such as a building, they knock it down using a bulldozer.

landfill [lǽndfìl] n. 쓰레기 매립지
A landfill is a large deep hole in which very large amounts of rubbish are buried.

seagull [síːgʌl] n. 갈매기
A seagull is a common kind of bird with white or gray feathers.

look ahead idiom (앞일을) 내다보다
If you look ahead, you think about what is going to happen in the future.

⁑ **blame** [bleim] v. ~을 탓하다, ~ 책임으로 보다
If you blame a person or thing for something bad, you believe or say that they are responsible for it or that they caused it.

⁑ **pause** [pɔːz] v. (말·일을 하다가) 잠시 멈추다; n. (말·행동 등의) 멈춤
If you pause while you are doing something, you stop for a short period and then continue.

* **laundry** [lɔ́ːndri] n. 세탁물; 세탁 (laundry basket n. 세탁물 바구니)
Laundry is used to refer to clothes, sheets, and towels that are about to be washed, are being washed, or have just been washed.

* **drip** [drip] v. 방울방울[뚝뚝] 흐르다
When something drips, drops of liquid fall from it.

* **risky** [ríski] a. 위험한
If an activity or action is risky, it is dangerous or likely to fail.

frown [fraun] v. 얼굴[눈살]을 찌푸리다; n. 찡그림, 찌푸림

When someone frowns, their eyebrows become drawn together, because they are annoyed or puzzled.

drain [drein] n. 배수구, 배수관; v. (액체를) 빼내다, 흘러나가다
(storm drain n. 빗물 배수관)

A drain is a small hole in a bath or sink which allows the water to flow away and into which you can put a plug.

current [kə́:rənt] n. (물·공기의) 흐름; a. 현재의, 지금의

A current is a steady and continuous flowing movement of some of the water in a river, lake, or sea.

harbor [há:rbər] n. 항구, 항만; 피난처, 은신처

A harbor is an area of the sea at the coast which is partly enclosed by land or strong walls, so that boats can be left there safely.

eventually [ivéntʃuəli] ad. 결국, 마침내

Eventually means at the end of a situation or process or as the final result of it.

shore [ʃɔ:r] n. (바다·호수의) 기슭, 해안, 호숫가

The shores or the shore of a sea, lake, or wide river is the land along the edge of it.

pluck [plʌk] v. (잡아 당겨) 빼내다; (머리카락·눈썹 등을) 뽑다

If you pluck something from somewhere, you take it between your fingers and pull it sharply from where it is.

in the first place idiom 애초에, 우선, 먼저

You say in the first place when you are talking about the beginning of a situation or about the situation as it was before a series of events.

fair [fɛər] a. 타당한, 온당한; 공정한, 공평한; n. 축제 마당; 박람회

Something or someone that is fair is reasonable, right, and just.

last resort [læst rizɔ́:rt] n. 마지막 수단

If you do something as a last resort, you do it because you can find no other way of getting out of a difficult situation or of solving a problem.

Chapter 4

1. **Who did Arthur first meet when he came home from school?**
   A. His mother
   B. His father
   C. His dog, Pal
   D. His sister, D.W.

2. **How did D.W. feel about Arthur's behavior?**
   A. She felt that he was acting weird.
   B. She felt that he was acting seriously.
   C. She felt that he had stress from school.
   D. She felt that he was excited about something.

3. **How did D.W. say that she knew when Arthur was worried?**

   A. Arthur got wrinkles when he was worried.

   B. Arthur started to shake when he was worried.

   C. Arthur blinked many times when he was worried.

   D. Arthur spoke very quickly when he was worried.

4. **What word on the envelope did D.W. not know?**

   A. Private

   B. Personal

   C. Confidence

   D. Confidential

5. **How did D.W. react when Arthur explained the story behind the envelope to her?**

   A. She told him that she would keep it a secret from their mom.

   B. She was genuinely concerned for Arthur.

   C. She started to sing that Arthur was in trouble.

   D. She thought that Arthur was lying about it.

Check Your Reading Speed

1분에 몇 단어를 읽는지 리딩 속도를 측정해보세요.

$$\frac{587 \text{ words}}{\text{reading time ( ) sec}} \times 60 = (\quad) \text{ WPM}$$

Build Your Vocabulary

driveway [dráivwèi] n. (도로에서 집·차고까지의) 진입로, 차도
A driveway is a piece of hard ground that leads from the road to the front of a house or other building.

disturb [distə́ːrb] v. (작업·수면 등을) 방해하다; (제자리에 있는 것을) 건드리다
If you disturb someone, you interrupt what they are doing and upset them.

bark [baːrk] v. (개가) 짖다; n. (개 등이) 짖는 소리
When a dog barks, it makes a short, loud noise, once or several times.

wag [wæg] v. (꼬리 등을) 흔들다, 흔들리다; n. 흔들기
When a dog wags its tail, it repeatedly waves its tail from side to side.

backpack [bǽkpæ̀k] n. 배낭
A backpack is a bag with straps that go over your shoulders, so that you can carry things on your back when you are walking or climbing.

counter [káuntər] n. (부엌의) 조리대; 계산대, 판매대; (요리점·간이 식당 등의) 카운터
A counter is a piece of furniture that stands at the side of a dining room, having shelves and drawers.

envelope [énvəlòup] n. 봉투
An envelope is the rectangular paper cover in which you send a letter to someone through the post.

stick out idiom 불쑥 나오다, 돌출하다
If something sticks out, it is further out than something else.

* **flap** [flæp] n. (봉투·호주머니 위에 달린 것 같은 납작한) 덮개; v. 퍼덕거리다, 퍼덕이다
A flap is something flat and broad that is attached at one side only and hangs loosely or covers an opening.

* **rinse** [rins] v. 씻다, 헹구다; n. (물에) 씻기, 헹구기
When you rinse something, you wash it in clean water in order to remove dirt or soap from it.

* **bury** [béri] v. 묻다, 매장하다
To bury something means to put it into a hole in the ground and cover it up with earth.

* **backyard** [bǽkjáːrd] n. 뒷마당, 뒤뜰
A backyard is an area of land at the back of a house.

whine [hwain] v. 낑낑거리다; 징징거리다, 우는 소리를 하다
If something or someone whines, they make a long, high-pitched noise, especially one which sounds sad or unpleasant.

복습 **disappoint** [dìsəpɔ́int] v. 실망시키다, 낙담시키다 (disappointment n. 실망, 낙심)
If things or people disappoint you, they are not as good as you had hoped, or do not do what you hoped they would do.

복습 **history** [hístəri] n. 역사(학)
History is a subject studied in schools, colleges, and universities that deals with events that have happened in the past.

make a face idiom 얼굴을 찌푸리다, 침울한 표정을 짓다
If you make a face, you twist your face to indicate a certain mental or emotional state.

* **fetch** [feʧ] v. (어디를 가서) 가지고 오다, 데리고 오다
If you fetch something or someone, you go and get them from the place where they are.

pantry [pǽntri] n. 식료품 저장실

A pantry is a small room or large cupboard in a house, usually near the
kitchen, where food is kept.

⁑ **actually** [ǽktʃuəli] ad. 실제로, 정말로

You use actually to indicate that a situation exists or happened, or to
emphasize that it is true.

⁑ **notice** [nóutis] v. ~을 의식하다, 주목하다, 관심을 기울이다; n. 신경 씀, 주목

If you notice something or someone, you become aware of them.

⁑ **lay** [lei] v. (laid–laid) 놓다, 눕히다; 알을 낳다

If you lay something somewhere, you put it there in a careful, gentle,
or neat way.

⁎ **remove** [rimúːv] v. (어떤 곳에서) 치우다; 없애다, 제거하다

If you remove something from a place, you take it away.

⁎ **whirl** [hwəːrl] v. 빙그르르[빙빙] 돌다; n. 빙빙 돌기, 선회하기

If something or someone whirls around or if you whirl them around, they
move around or turn around very quickly.

⁎ **doorway** [dɔ́ːrwèi] n. 문간, 현관, 출입구

A doorway is a space in a wall where a door opens and closes.

⁎ **silly** [síli] n. 바보; a. 어리석은, 바보 같은

If you call someone silly, you mean that they are foolish, childish, or
ridiculous.

⁑ **shout** [ʃaut] v. 외치다, 소리치다; n. 외침, 고함

If you shout, you say something very loudly, usually because you want
people a long distance away to hear you or because you are angry.

⁑ **lean** [liːn] v. 기울다, (몸을) 숙이다

When you lean in a particular direction, you bend your body in that
direction.

⁎ **dumb** [dʌm] a. 멍청한, 바보 같은; 벙어리의, 말을 못 하는

If you call a person dumb, you mean that they are stupid or foolish.

^{복습}**bother** [báðər] v. 신경 쓰다, 애를 쓰다; 신경 쓰이게 하다, 괴롭히다; n. 성가심

If you do not bother to do something or if you do not bother with it, you do not do it, consider it, or use it because you think it is unnecessary or because you are too lazy.

★ **boring** [bɔ́:riŋ] a. 재미없는, 지루한

Someone or something boring is so dull and uninteresting that they make people tired and impatient.

★ **weird** [wiəːrd] a. 기이한, 기묘한

If you describe something or someone as weird, you mean that they are strange.

★ **straighten** [streitn] v. 똑바르게 하다, 곧게 하다

If you straighten something, you make it tidy or put it in its proper position.

^{복습}**fold** [fould] v. (손·팔·다리를) 끼다, 포개다; 접다, 접어 포개다

If you fold your arms or hands, you bring them together and cross or link them, for example over your chest.

^{복습}**stare** [stɛər] v. 응시하다, 뚫어지게 보다

If you stare at someone or something, you look at them for a long time.

★ **fool** [fu:l] v. 속이다, 기만하다; n. 바보

If someone fools you, they deceive or trick you.

★ **blink** [bliŋk] v. 눈을 깜박거리다; (등불·별 등이) 깜박이다; n. 깜박거림

When you blink or when you blink your eyes, you shut your eyes and very quickly open them again.

^{복습}**nod** [nad] v. (고개를) 끄덕이다, 끄덕여 나타내다; n. (고개를) 끄덕임

If you nod, you move your head downward and upward to show agreement, understanding, or approval.

★ **wrinkle** [riŋkl] n. (얼굴의) 주름; n. (얼굴에) 주름을 잡다, 찡그리다

Wrinkles are lines which form on someone's face as they grow old.

^{복습} surprise [sərpráiz] v. 놀라게 하다, 경악하게 하다 (surprised a. 매우 놀란)
If you surprise someone, you give them, tell them, or do something they are not expecting.

forget [fərgét] v. 잊다, 잊어버리다
If you forget something or forget how to do something, you cannot think of it or think how to do it, although you knew it or knew how to do it in the past.

^{복습} sigh [sai] v. 한숨 쉬다; n. 한숨, 탄식
When you sigh, you let out a deep breath, as a way of expressing feelings such as disappointment, tiredness, or pleasure.

regular [régjulər] a. 규칙적인, 정기적인; 잦은, 주기적인
Regular events have equal amounts of time between them, so that they happen, for example, at the same time each day or each week.

handle [hændl] v. (상황·사람·작업·감정을) 다루다; n. 손잡이
If you say that someone can handle a problem or situation, you mean that they have the ability to deal with it successfully.

come on idiom 자, 어서, 그러지 말고
People say 'come on' to encourage someone to do something.

spill the beans idiom 비밀을 말하다
If you spill the beans, you tell someone something that people have been trying to keep secret.

^{복습} principal [prínsəpəl] n. 교장, 학장, 총장; a. 주요한, 주된
The principal of a school is the person in charge of the school.

^{복습} private [práivət] a. 사적인, 개인적인
Your private things belong only to you, or may only be used by you.

^{복습} confidential [kànfədénʃəl] a. 비밀의, 기밀의; 은밀한
Information that is confidential is meant to be kept secret or private.

복습 **frown** [fraun] v. 얼굴[눈살]을 찌푸리다; n. 찡그림, 찌푸림
When someone frowns, their eyebrows become drawn together, because they are annoyed or puzzled.

★ **skip** [skip] v. 깡충깡충[팔짝팔짝] 뛰다; (일을) 거르다
If you skip along, you move almost as if you are dancing, with a series of little jumps from one foot to the other.

for once idiom 이번에는, 이번만은
If you say you do something for once, you mean that you do it on this occasion in contrast that you usually do not.

★★★ **argue** [áːrgjuː] v. 언쟁을 하다, 다투다
If one person argues with another, they speak angrily to each other about something that they disagree about.

Chapter 5

1. Why did D.W. stop singing?

    A. She had bumped into a table.

    B. She had bumped into her mother.

    C. She had run out of breath.

    D. She had grown tired of the song.

2. What did Mrs. Read do for a job?

    A. She was an accountant.

    B. She was a caterer.

    C. She was a secretary.

    D. She was an actress.

3. **What did Mrs. Read notice on the table and move?**

    A. She noticed Arthur's homework.

    B. She noticed Arthur's backpack.

    C. She noticed the envelope.

    D. She noticed Pal's food dish.

4. **What did Mr. Read carry into the kitchen?**

    A. A container of whipped cream

    B. A bundle of letters

    C. A new dish for Pal

    D. A new dessert for his family

5. **What happened to the envelope that Arthur brought home?**

    A. Arthur dropped it in the wastebasket on purpose.

    B. Mrs. Read read it immediately and tossed it into the wastebasket.

    C. Mrs. Read dropped it into the wastebasket after Arthur gave it to her.

    D. Mrs. Read was distracted and it fell into the wastebasket.

Check Your Reading Speed

1분에 몇 단어를 읽는지 리딩 속도를 측정해보세요.

$$\frac{556 \text{ words}}{\text{reading time ( ) sec}} \times 60 = (\qquad) \text{ WPM}$$

Build Your Vocabulary

⋆ **bump** [bʌmp] v. (~에) 부딪치다; n. 쿵, 탁(단단한 것에 부딪치는 소리)
If you bump into something or someone, you accidentally hit them while you are moving.

⋆ **afford** [əfɔ́:rd] v. (~을 할 금전적·시간적) 여유가 되다, 형편이 되다
If you cannot afford something, you do not have enough money to pay for it.

⋆ **traffic light** [trǽfik làit] n. (교통) 신호등
Traffic lights are sets of red, amber, and green lights at the places where roads meet. They control the traffic by signaling.

⋆ **accountant** [əkáuntənt] n. 회계원, 회계사
An accountant is a person whose job is to keep financial accounts.

frazzled [frǽzld] a. 기진맥진한
If you are frazzled, you are exhausted physically or emotionally.

⋆ **tax** [tæks] n. 세금; v. 세금을 부과하다, 과세하다
Tax is an amount of money that you have to pay to the government so that it can pay for public services.

⋆ **weird** [wiə:rd] a. 기이한, 기묘한
If you describe something or someone as weird, you mean that they are strange.

hush [hʌʃ] int. 쉿, 조용히 해; v. ~을 조용히 시키다; n. 침묵, 고요
You say 'Hush!' to someone when you are asking or telling them to be quiet.

counter [káuntər] n. (부엌의) 조리대; 계산대, 판매대; (요리점·간이 식당 등의) 카운터
A counter is a piece of furniture that stands at the side of a dining room, having shelves and drawers.

cringe [krindʒ] v. (겁이 나서) 움츠리다, 움찔하다
If you cringe at something, you feel embarrassed or disgusted, and perhaps show this feeling in your expression or by making a slight movement.

envelope [énvəlòup] n. 봉투
An envelope is the rectangular paper cover in which you send a letter to someone through the post.

fold [fould] v. (손·팔·다리를) 끼다, 포개다; 접다, 접어 포개다
If you fold your arms or hands, you bring them together and cross or link them, for example over your chest.

let out idiom (울음소리·신음소리 등을) 내다
If you let out a cry or a sigh, you make a sound.

breath [breθ] n. 숨, 호흡
Your breath is the air that you let out through your mouth when you breathe.

honestly [ánistli] ad. 정말로, 진짜로; 솔직히
You use honestly to emphasize that you are telling the truth and that you want people to believe you.

expect [ikspékt] v. 요구하다, 바라다; 예상하다, 기대하다
If you expect something, or expect a person to do something, you believe that it is your right to have that thing, or the person's duty to do it for you.

fidget [fídʒit] v. (초조·지루함·흥분 등으로) 꼼지락거리다, 가만히 못 있다

If you fidget, you keep moving your hands or feet slightly or changing your position slightly, for example because you are nervous, bored, or excited.

dial [daiəl] v. 다이얼을 돌리다, 전화를 걸다; n. (시계·계기 등의) 문자반, 눈금판

If you dial, you turn the dial or press the buttons on a telephone in order to phone someone.

secretary [sékrətèri] n. 비서; 총무, 서기

A secretary is a person who is employed to do office work, such as typing letters, answering phone calls, and arranging meetings.

glance [glæns] v. 흘낏 보다, 잠깐 보다; n. 흘낏 봄

If you glance at something or someone, you look at them very quickly and then look away again immediately.

pale [peil] a. 창백한, 핼쑥한; (색깔이) 엷은

If someone looks pale, their face looks a lighter color than usual, usually because they are ill, frightened, or shocked.

drawer [drɔːr] n. 서랍

A drawer is part of a desk, chest, or other piece of furniture that is shaped like a box and is designed for putting things in.

bundle [bʌndl] n. 꾸러미, 묶음, 보따리

A bundle of things is a number of them that are tied together or wrapped in a cloth or bag so that they can be carried or stored.

whip [hwip] v. (크림 등을) 휘저어 거품을 내다; 채찍질하다
(whipped cream n. 거품을 낸 크림)

When you whip something liquid such as cream or an egg, you stir it very fast until it is thick or stiff.

scrape [skreip] v. (무엇을 떼어 내기 위해) 긁다, 긁어내다; n. 긁기

If you scrape something from a surface, you remove it, especially by pulling a sharp object over the surface.

experiment [ikspérəmənt] v. (과학적인) 실험을 하다; n. (과학적인) 실험
To experiment means to try out a new idea or method to see what it is like and what effects it has.

dessert [dizə́:rt] n. 디저트, 후식
Dessert is something sweet, such as fruit or a pudding, that you eat at the end of a meal.

catering [kéitəriŋ] n. (행사·연회 등을 대상으로 하는) 음식 공급
Catering is the activity of providing food and drink for a large number of people, for example at weddings and parties.

sigh [sai] v. 한숨 쉬다; n. 한숨, 탄식
When you sigh, you let out a deep breath, as a way of expressing feelings such as disappointment, tiredness, or pleasure.

piecrust [páikrʌ̀st] n. 파이 껍질
Piecrust is the pastry shell of a pie.

survive [sərváiv] v. 살아남다, 생존하다
If a person or living thing survives in a dangerous situation such as an accident or an illness, they do not die.

wastebasket [wéistbæskit] n. 휴지통
A wastebasket is a container for rubbish, especially paper, which is usually placed on the floor in the corner of a room or next to a desk.

put aside idiom ~을 한쪽으로 치우다
If you put something aside, you place it to one side.

bill [bil] n. 청구서, 계산서; 지폐; v. 청구서를 보내다, 청구하다
A bill is a written statement of money that you owe for goods or services.

paperwork [péipərwə̀:rk] n. 서류 사무, 문서 업무
Paperwork is the routine part of a job which involves writing or dealing with letters, reports, and records.

flip [flip] v. (책장을) 휙휙 넘기다; 홱 뒤집(히)다, 휙 젖히다; n. 톡 던지기; 공중제비

If you flip through the pages of a book, for example, you quickly turn over the pages in order to find a particular one or to get an idea of the contents.

magazine [mǽgəzíːn] n. 잡지

A magazine is a publication with a paper cover which is issued regularly, usually every week or every month, and which contains articles, stories, photographs, and advertisements.

due [djuː] a. ～하기로 되어 있는; ～로 인한

If something is due at a particular time, it is expected to happen, be done, or arrive at that time.

increase [inkríːs] v. 증가하다, 늘리다, 불리다; n. 증가, 증대 (increasing a. 증가하는)

If something increases or you increase it, it becomes greater in number, level, or amount.

doom [duːm] n. (피할 수 없는) 비운; v. 불행한 운명[결말]을 맞게 하다

If you have a sense or feeling of doom, you feel that things are going very badly and are likely to get even worse.

edge [edʒ] v. 조금씩[살살] 움직이다, 이동시키다; n. 끝, 가장자리, 모서리

If someone or something edges somewhere, they move very slowly in that direction.

stove [stouv] n. (요리용 가스·전기) 레인지; 스토브, 난로

A stove is a piece of equipment which provides heat, either for cooking or for heating a room.

bubble [bʌbl] v. 거품이 일다, 보글보글 끓다; n. 거품 (bubble over idiom 넘치다)

When a liquid bubbles, bubbles move in it, for example because it is boiling or moving quickly.

hang up idiom 전화를 끊다, 수화기를 놓다; 중지하다

If you hang up on someone, you end telephone conversation with them.

teeter [tí:tər] v. (넘어질 듯이) 불안정하게 서다, 위아래로 움직이다
If someone or something teeters, they shake in an unsteady way, and seem to be about to lose their balance and fall over.

slump [slʌmp] v. 털썩 앉다; (가치·수량·가격 등이) 급감하다; n. 급감, 급락; 폭락
If you slump somewhere, you fall or sit down there heavily, for example because you are very tired or you feel ill.

⚡ **relief** [rilí:f] n. 안도, 안심; (고통·불안 등의) 경감
If you feel a sense of relief, you feel happy because something unpleasant has not happened or is no longer happening.

＊ **innocent** [ínəsənt] a. 아무 잘못이 없는, 무죄인, 결백한
If someone is innocent, they did not commit a crime which they have been accused of.

복습 **trash** [træʃ] n. 쓰레기; v. 부수다, 엉망으로 만들다
Trash consists of unwanted things or waste material such as used paper, empty containers and bottles, and waste food.

⚡ **guide** [gaid] v. 인도하다; 안내하여 데려가다; n. 안내(서), 가이드
If something guides you somewhere, it gives you the information you need in order to go in the right direction.

복습 **fate** [feit] n. 운명, 숙명
Fate is a power that some people believe controls and decides everything that happens, in a way that cannot be prevented or changed.

＊ **destiny** [déstəni] n. 운명
Destiny is the force which some people believe controls the things that happen to you in your life.

Chapter 6

1. How did Arthur feel at dinner?

   A. He felt very hungry and ate quickly.

   B. He felt like he had a stomachache and left early.

   C. He was distracted by the envelope and ate little.

   D. He did not eat at all because it was his least favorite food.

2. What did Arthur usually do with his potato puffs and green beans?

   A. He lined up the potato puffs like alligator and the beans like a castle wall.

   B. He piled up the potato puffs like a castle wall and the beans like alligators.

   C. He arranged them so that they looked like little shredded carpets.

   D. He stamped both of them down together with his fork.

3. **What did Mr. Read say was different about his school days?**

   A. He said that Arthur had it much easier.

   B. He said that he used to have more projects.

   C. He said that they did not have any tests.

   D. He said that Arthur had more choices.

4. **What did Mr. Read say about history?**

   A. He said that it was not interesting.

   B. He said that it was boring.

   C. He said that it was important.

   D. He said that math was more useful.

5. **What did Arthur give his mother at dinner?**

   A. He gave his mother his thanks for the dinner.

   B. He gave his mother free time by doing the dishes.

   C. He gave his mother the envelope that Mr. Haney had given him.

   D. He gave his mother his report card that he had received at school.

Check Your Reading Speed

1분에 몇 단어를 읽는지 리딩 속도를 측정해보세요.

$$\frac{505 \text{ words}}{\text{reading time ( ) sec}} \times 60 = (\quad) \text{ WPM}$$

Build Your Vocabulary

✱ **swallow** [swálou] v. 삼키다, 목구멍으로 넘기다; (초조해서) 마른침을 삼키다
If you swallow something, you cause it to go from your mouth down into your stomach.

✱ **concentrate** [kánsəntrèit] v. 집중하다, 전념하다
If you concentrate on something, you give all your attention to it.

복습 **envelope** [énvəlòup] n. 봉투
An envelope is the rectangular paper cover in which you send a letter to someone through the post.

peek [piːk] v. 살짝 들여다보다; (재빨리) 훔쳐보다; n. 엿보기
If you peek at something or someone, you have a quick look at them.

복습 **wastebasket** [wéistbæskit] n. 휴지통
A wastebasket is a container for rubbish, especially paper, which is usually placed on the floor in the corner of a room or next to a desk.

✱ **cheer** [tʃiər] v. 응원하다, 환호성을 지르다; n. 환호(성)
If you are cheered by something, it makes you happier or less worried.

복습 **edge** [edʒ] n. 끝, 가장자리, 모서리; v. 조금씩[살살] 움직이다, 이동시키다
The edge of something is the place or line where it stops, or the part of it that is furthest from the middle.

복습 **plate** [pleit] n. (둥그런) 접시, 그릇
A plate is a round or oval flat dish that is used to hold food.

crescent [kresnt] n. 초승달 모양(의 것)

A crescent is a curved shape that is wider in the middle than at its ends, like the shape of the moon during its first and last quarters.

★ **pile** [pail] v. 쌓다, 포개다; n. 쌓아 놓은 것, 더미

If you pile things somewhere, you put them there so that they form a pile.

★ **bean** [bi:n] n. 콩

Beans such as green beans, French beans, or broad beans are the seeds of a climbing plant or the long thin cases which contain those seeds.

★ **alligator** [ǽligèitər] n. 악어

An alligator is a large reptile with short legs, a long tail and very powerful jaws.

moat [mout] n. 호, 해자(성 주위에 둘러 판 못)

A moat is a deep, wide channel dug round a place such as a castle and filled with water, in order to protect the place from attack.

복습 **stamp** [stæmp] v. (도장·스탬프 등을) 찍다; (발을) 구르다; n. 우표; 도장

If you stamp a mark or word on an object, you press the mark or word onto the object using a stamp or other device.

★ **shred** [ʃred] v. (갈가리) 자르다, 찢다; n. (가늘고 작은) 조각 (shredded a. 잘게 조각난)

If you shred something such as food or paper, you cut it or tear it into very small, narrow pieces.

wear and tear idiom (일상적인 사용에 의한) 마모, 손상

Wear and tear is the damage or change that is caused to something when it is being used normally.

★ **confuse** [kənfjú:z] v. 어리둥절하게 하다, 혼동하다 (confused a. 당황한, 어리둥절한)

To confuse someone means to make it difficult for them to know exactly what is happening or what to do.

mash [mæʃ] v. (음식을 부드럽게) 으깨다

If you mash something, you crush it so that it forms a soft mass.

★ **bite** [bait] n. 한 입(의 분량); 물기, 물어뜯기; v. 묻다, 물어뜯다
A bite of something, especially food, is the action of biting it.

복습 **help oneself** idiom 마음대로 집어먹다, 자유로이 먹다
If someone tells you to help yourself, they are telling you politely to serve
yourself anything you want or to take anything you want.

★ **awful** [ɔ́:fəl] a. 지독한, 대단한; 무서운 (awfully ad. (구어) 대단히, 몹시)
If you say that something is awful, you mean that it is extremely
unpleasant, shocking, or bad.

squirm [skwə:rm] v. (초조하거나 불편하거나 하여 몸을) 꿈틀대다, 꼼지락대다
If you squirm, you move your body from side to side, usually because
you are nervous or uncomfortable.

★ **definite** [défənit] a. 확실한, 확고한; 분명한, 뚜렷한 (definitely ad. 확실히, 명확히)
If something such as a decision or an arrangement is definite, It is firm
and clear, and unlikely to be changed.

swap [swap] v. (어떤 것을 주고 그 대신 다른 것으로) 바꾸다
If you swap something with someone, you give it to them and receive
a different thing in exchange.

domination [dàmənéiʃən] n. 지배, 통치
Domination is an act of controlling a country, person, or area with power
over them.

★★ **matter** [mǽtər] v. 중요하다; 문제되다; n. (고려하거나 처리해야 할) 문제
If you say that something does matter, you mean that it is important to
you because it does have an effect on you or on a particular situation.

복습 **catering** [kéitəriŋ] n. (행사·연회 등을 대상으로 하는) 음식 공급
Catering is the activity of providing food and drink for a large number
of people, for example at weddings and parties.

★ **advertising** [ǽdvərtàiziŋ] n. 광고(하기); 광고업
Advertising is the activity of creating advertisements and making sure
people see them.

✮ **recipe** [résəpi] n. 조리법, 요리법
A recipe is a list of ingredients and a set of instructions that tell you how to cook something.

✮ **create** [krieit] v. 창조하다, 창작하다
To create something means to cause it to happen or exist.

✮ **meal** [miːl] n. (아침·점심·저녁의) 식사
A meal is an occasion when people sit down and eat, usually at a regular time.

✮ **historical** [histɔ́ːrikəl] a. 역사적, 역사상의
Historical people, situations, or things existed in the past and are considered to be a part of history.

✮ **theme** [θiːm] n. 주제, 테마
A theme in a piece of writing, a talk, or a discussion is an important idea or subject that runs through it.

make sense idiom 뜻이 통하다, 도리에 맞다
If something makes sense, it has a meaning that you can easily understand.

★ **handy** [hǽndi] a. 편리한, 유용한 (come in handy idiom 여러 모로 편리하다)
If something comes in handy, it is useful in a particular situation.

✮ **bowl** [boul] n. 사발, 그릇
A bowl is a round container with a wide uncovered top.

while one is at it idiom 말이 나온 김에, ~하는 김에
While you are at it means while you are doing it.

★ **barely** [bέərli] ad. 간신히, 가까스로, 빠듯하게
You use barely to say that something is only just true or only just the case.

for now idiom 우선은, 현재로는, 당분간은
For now means for a period of time from now until something else happens.

Chapter 7

1. Which of the following was NOT a homework question that made Arthur think of the envelope?

A. A problem involving cutting a rectangle in half

B. A problem involving a mailbag filled with letters

C. A problem involving a word that rhymed with rope and hope

D. A problem involving a letter on a map

2. What did Arthur imagine as he drew the rectangle?

A. He imagined being mailed in a large envelope on a ship.

B. He imagined being chased by a large envelope down a hill.

C. He imagined being crushed by a large envelope falling from the sky.

D. He imagined being yelled at by a large envelope in a forest.

3. **How did Arthur feel when he saw baby Kate sleeping?**

    A. He thought about taking a nap just like a baby.

    B. He thought that babies were too cute to be in trouble.

    C. He thought that babies were lucky not to worry.

    D. He thought that he could be a good brother.

4. **What were D.W. and her father watching?**

    A. The Karaoke Kittens

    B. The Crazy Cats

    C. The Dangerous Dogs

    D. The Singing Snakes

5. **How does the commercial about headaches make Arthur feel?**

    A. He wanted his headache to go away.

    B. He wanted to open the envelope.

    C. He wanted to watch more TV.

    D. He wanted a pill to solve his problem.

Check Your Reading Speed

1분에 몇 단어를 읽는지 리딩 속도를 측정해보세요.

$$\frac{501 \text{ words}}{\text{reading time (} \quad \text{) sec}} \times 60 = (\quad) \text{ WPM}$$

Build Your Vocabulary

★ **rhyme** [raim] v. (두 단어나 음절이) 운이 맞다, 운을 맞추다; n. (시의) 운

If one word rhymes with another or if two words rhyme, they have a very similar sound.

★ **switch** [switʃ] v. 전환하다, 바꾸다; n. 스위치

If you switch to something different, for example to a different system, task, or subject of conversation, you change to it from what you were doing or saying before.

복습 **involve** [inválv] v. 포함하다; (상황·사건·활동이 사람을) 관련시키다

If a situation or activity involves something, that thing is a necessary part or consequence of it.

복습 **rectangle** [réktæŋgl] n. 직사각형

A rectangle is a four-sided shape whose corners are all ninety degree angles. Each side of a rectangle is the same length as the one opposite to it.

복습 **envelope** [énvəlòup] n. 봉투

An envelope is the rectangular paper cover in which you send a letter to someone through the post.

mailbag [méilbæg] n. 우편(물) 가방

A mailbag is a large bag that is used by postal workers for carrying mail.

★★★ **mention** [ménʃən] n. 언급, 거론; v. 말하다, 언급하다

A mention is a reference to something or someone.

doodle [duːdl] v. (지루해 하거나 딴 생각을 하면서) 뭔가를 끼적거리다
When someone doodles, they draw a pattern or picture that you draw when you are bored or thinking about something else.

edge [edʒ] n. 끝, 가장자리, 모서리; v. 조금씩[살살] 움직이다, 이동시키다
The edge of something is the place or line where it stops, or the part of it that is furthest from the middle.

enormous [inɔ́ːrməs] a. 막대한, 거대한
You can use enormous to emphasize the great degree or extent of something.

chase [ʧeis] v. 뒤쫓다, 추적하다; n. 추적, 추격
If you chase someone, or chase after them, you run after them or follow them quickly in order to catch or reach them.

tumble [tʌmbl] v. 굴러 떨어지다, 굴리다; n. (갑자기) 굴러 떨어짐
If someone or something tumbles somewhere, they fall there with a rolling or bouncing movement.

end over end idiom 빙글빙글 회전하여
If something tumbles end over end, it falls with a rolling movement.

barely [béərli] ad. 간신히, 가까스로, 빠듯하게
You use barely to say that something is only just true or only just the case.

fit [fit] v. (모양·크기가 어떤 사람·사물에) 맞다
If something fits, it is the right size and shape to go onto a person's body or onto a particular object.

flatten [flǽtn] v. 납작해지다, 반반하게 만들다
If you flatten something or if it flattens, it becomes flat or flatter.

huff and puff idiom (몹시 지쳐서) 헉헉거리다
If you huff and puff, you breathe heavily while making a great physical effort.

huff [hʌf] v. (화가 나서) 씩씩거리다
If you huff, you indicate that you are annoyed or offended about something.

★ **puff** [pʌf] v. 숨을 헐떡거리다; (담배·파이프 등을) 뻐끔뻐끔 피우다
If you are puffing, you are breathing loudly and quickly with your mouth open because you are out of breath after a lot of physical effort.

복습 **shape** [ʃeip] n. 모양, 형태; v. (어떤) 모양[형태]으로 만들다
(in good shape idiom (몸의) 상태가 좋은)
If someone or something is in good shape, they are in a good state of health or in a good condition.

★ **rub** [rʌb] v. 문지르다, 비비다; n. 문지르기, 비비기
If you rub a part of your body, you move your hand or fingers backward and forward over it while pressing firmly.

복습 **peek** [piːk] n. 엿보기; v. (재빨리) 훔쳐보다; 살짝 들여다보다
If you take a peek at something or someone, you have a quick look at them.

★ **mutter** [mʌ́tər] v. 중얼거리다, 불평하다; n. 중얼거림, 불평
If you mutter, you speak very quietly so that you cannot easily be heard, often because you are complaining about something.

복습 **history** [hístəri] n. 역사(학)
History is a subject studied in schools, colleges, and universities that deals with events that have happened in the past.

★ **cute** [kjuːt] a. 귀여운
Something or someone that is cute is very pretty or attractive, or is intended to appear pretty or attractive.

diaper [dáiəpər] n. 기저귀
A diaper is a piece of soft towel or paper, which you fasten round a baby's bottom in order to soak up its urine and feces.

blanket [blǽŋkit] n. 담요, 모포
A blanket is a large square or rectangular piece of thick cloth, especially one which you put on a bed to keep you warm.

slip [slip] v. 미끄러지다; 슬며시 가다
If something slips, it slides out of place or out of your hand.

sigh [sai] v. 한숨 쉬다; n. 한숨, 탄식
When you sigh, you let out a deep breath, as a way of expressing feelings such as disappointment, tiredness, or pleasure.

chew [ʧuː] v. 씹다, 물어뜯다, 깨물다
If you chew on something, you bite it continuously, especially because you are nervous or to test your teeth.

hum [hʌm] v. 콧노래를 부르다, (노래를) 흥얼거리다; n. 웅웅거리는 소리
If something hums, it makes a low continuous noise.

tiptoe [típtòu] v. 발끝으로 살금살금 걷다
If you tiptoe somewhere, you walk there very quietly without putting your heels on the floor when you walk.

kitten [kitn] n. 새끼 고양이
A kitten is a very young cat.

straw [strɔː] n. 짚, 밀짚; 빨대 (straw hat n. 밀짚모자)
Straw consists of the dried, yellowish stalks from crops such as wheat or barley.

in a line idiom 한 줄로, 정렬하여
If one object is in a line with others, they are arranged in one line.

in time idiom 박자를 맞추어; 시간에 맞춰, 제때에
If you play, sing, or dance in time to music, you do it at the right speed.

point out idiom ~을 지적하다
If you point out a fact or mistake, you tell someone about it or draw their attention to it.

practice [prǽktis] n. 연습, 훈련; 실행, 실천; v. 연습하다; 실행하다
Practice means doing something regularly in order to be able to do it better.

commercial [kəmə́:rʃəl] n. (텔레비전·라디오의) 광고; a. 상업의, 무역의
A commercial is an advertisement that is broadcast on television or radio.

get someone down idiom ~을 우울하게 만들다
If something gets you down, it makes you feel unhappy or depressed.

nod [nad] v. (고개를) 끄덕이다, 끄덕여 나타내다; n. (고개를) 끄덕임
If you nod, you move your head downward and upward to show agreement, understanding, or approval.

pound [paund] v. (머리가) 지끈거리다; (가슴이) 쿵쿵 뛰다; 치다, 두드리다
If your head pounds, you have a headache with a throbbing pain.

cradle [kreidl] v. (안전하게 보호하듯이) 떠받치다, 살짝 안다; n. 유아용 침대
If you cradle someone or something in your arms or hands, you hold them carefully and gently.

headache [hédèik] n. 두통, 머리가 아픔
If you have a headache, you have a pain in your head.

relief [rilí:f] n. (고통·불안 등의) 경감; 안도, 안심
If something provides relief from pain or distress, it stops the pain or distress.

pill [pil] n. 알약
Pills are small solid round masses of medicine or vitamins that you swallow without chewing.

get rid of ~ idiom ~을 쫓아버리다, 없애다
When you get rid of something that you do not want or do not like, you take action so that you no longer have it or suffer from it.

admit [ædmít] v. 인정하다
If you admit that something bad, unpleasant, or embarrassing is true, you agree, often unwillingly, that it is true.

fur [fəːr] n. (동물의) 털

Fur is the thick and usually soft hair that grows on the bodies of many mammals.

Chapter 8

1. Which of the following did NOT remind Arthur of envelopes?

    A. His pillow

    B. His teeth

    C. His computer

    D. The wallpaper

2. Why did D.W. want to talk to Arthur?

    A. She wanted to know about the trouble Arthur was in.

    B. She wanted to know if Arthur had another envelope.

    C. She wanted Arthur to help her after she had a nightmare.

    D. She wanted to offer advice for helping him with the trouble in the envelope.

3. **Why did Arthur's mother not mention the envelope to him?**

    A. She had given the envelope to Arthur's father instead.

    B. She had read it, but it did not concern Arthur.

    C. She had read it but was too busy to talk to Arthur.

    D. She had not seen it yet.

4. **What did Arthur do with the envelope in his dream?**

    A. He put it in a paper shredder and destroyed it.

    B. He put it in the tub and drew the shower curtain.

    C. He buried it in the backyard.

    D. He tried to flush it down the toilet.

5. **What was inside the envelope in Arthur's dream?**

    A. D.W. telling Arthur that he had tricked her

    B. Arthur's mother yelling at him for hiding the envelope

    C. Mr. Ratburn telling Arthur to come to summer school

    D. Mr. Haney telling Arthur to give his mother the letter

Check Your Reading Speed

1분에 몇 단어를 읽는지 리딩 속도를 측정해보세요.

$$\frac{497 \text{ words}}{\text{reading time (} \quad \text{) sec}} \times 60 = (\quad) \text{ WPM}$$

Build Your Vocabulary

＊pillow [pílou] n. 베개; 머리 받침대

A pillow is a rectangular cushion which you rest your head on when you are in bed.

notice [nóutis] v. ~을 의식하다, 주목하다, 관심을 기울이다; n. 신경 씀, 주목

If you notice something or someone, you become aware of them.

stuff [stʌf] v. 채워 넣다, 채우다; n. 것(들), 물건, 물질

If you stuff a container or space with something, you fill it with something or with a quantity of things until it is full.

envelope [énvəlòup] n. 봉투

An envelope is the rectangular paper cover in which you send a letter to someone through the post.

＊brush [brʌʃ] v. 솔질을 하다; (솔이나 손으로) 털다

(brush one's teeth idiom 이를 닦다, 양치질을 하다)

If you brush your teeth, you clean your teeth with toothbrush and toothpaste.

＊＊square [skwɛəːr] a. 정사각형 모양의; n. 정사각형

A square is a shape with four sides that are all the same length and four corners that are all right angles.

＊row [rou] ① n. 열, 줄; 좌석 줄 ② v. 노[배]를 젓다

A row of things or people is a number of them arranged in a line.

64

wallpaper [wɔ́ːlpéipər] n. 벽지
Wallpaper is thick colored or patterned paper that is used for covering and decorating the walls of rooms.

carpeting [káːrpitiŋ] n. 카펫류
You use carpeting to refer to a carpet, or to the type of material that is used to make carpets.

^{복습} **blanket** [blǽŋkit] n. 담요, 모포
A blanket is a large square or rectangular piece of thick cloth, especially one which you put on a bed to keep you warm.

^{복습} **shape** [ʃeip] n. 모양, 형태; v. (어떤) 모양[형태]으로 만들다
The shape of an object, a person, or an area is the appearance of their outside edges or surfaces, for example whether they are round, square, curved, or fat.

have something on the brain idiom ~이 머리에서 떠나지 않다, ~에 늘 정신이 팔려 있다
If you have someone or something on the brain, you think or talk a lot about them.

^{★★★} **awake** [əwéik] a. (아직) 잠들지 않은, 깨어 있는
Someone who is awake is not sleeping.

^{복습} **doorway** [dɔ́ːrwèi] n. 문간, 현관, 출입구
A doorway is a space in a wall where a door opens and closes.

sound asleep idiom 깊이 잠들다
If someone is sound asleep, they are sleeping very deeply.

[★] **convince** [kənvíns] v. 확신시키다, 납득시키다; 설득하다 (convinced a. 확신하는)
If someone or something convinces you of something, they make you believe that it is true or that it exists.

^{복습} **honestly** [ánistli] ad. 솔직히; 정말로, 진짜로
You use honestly to emphasize that you are telling the truth and that you want people to believe you.

mention [ménʃən] v. 말하다, 언급하다; n. 언급, 거론

If you mention something, you say something about it, usually briefly.

disappoint [dìsəpɔ́int] v. 실망시키다, 낙담시키다 (disappointed a. 실망한, 좌절된)

If things or people disappoint you, they are not as good as you had hoped, or do not do what you hoped they would do.

stare [stɛər] v. 응시하다, 뚫어지게 보다

If you stare at someone or something, you look at them for a long time.

ceiling [síːliŋ] n. 천장

A ceiling is the horizontal surface that forms the top part or roof inside a room.

strictly [stríktli] ad. 엄밀히, 정확히; 엄격히, 엄하게

You use strictly to emphasize that something is of one particular type, or intended for one particular thing or person, rather than any other.

wastebasket [wéistbæskit] n. 휴지통

A wastebasket is a container for rubbish, especially paper, which is usually placed on the floor in the corner of a room or next to a desk.

rustle [rʌsl] v. 바스락거리다; n. 바스락거리는 소리

If things such as paper or leaves rustle, or if you rustle them, they move about and make a soft, dry sound.

downstairs [dáunstéərz] ad. 아래층으로, 아래층에서; n. 아래층

If something or someone is downstairs in a building, they are on the ground floor or on a lower floor than you.

bounce [bauns] v. 튀다, 튀게 하다; 급히 움직이다, 뛰어다니다; n. 튐, 바운드

If something bounces off a surface or is bounced off it, it reaches the surface and is reflected back.

flap [flæp] v. 퍼덕거리다, 퍼덕이다; n. (봉투·호주머니 위에 달린 것 같은 납작한) 덮개

If something such as a piece of cloth or paper flaps or if you flap it, it moves quickly up and down or from side to side.

drag [dræg] v. (무거운 것을) 끌다, 끌어당기다; (발 등을) 질질 끌다

If you drag something, you pull it along the ground, often with difficulty.

hoist [hɔist] v. (흔히 밧줄이나 장비를 이용하여) 들어올리다; n. 승강 장치
If you hoist something heavy somewhere, you lift it or pull it up there.

tub [tʌb] n. 목욕통, 욕조; 통
A tub is a long, usually rectangular container which you fill with water and sit in to wash your body.

tremble [trembl] v. (몸을) 떨다, 떨리다
If something trembles, it shakes slightly.

flee [fliː] v. (fled–fled) 달아나다, 도망치다
If you flee from something or someone, or flee a person or thing, you escape from them.

grab [græb] v. 부여잡다, 움켜쥐다; n. 부여잡기
If you grab something, you take it or pick it up suddenly and roughly.

wriggle [rigl] v. (몸·몸의 일부를) 꿈틀거리다; n. 꿈틀거리기
If you wriggle or wriggle part of your body, you twist and turn with quick movements.

pop [pap] v. 불쑥 나타나다; 뻥 하고 터뜨리다; n. 뻥[탁] 하는 소리; 발포
If something pops out, it suddenly comes out from a place.

chimney [tʃímni] n. 굴뚝
A chimney is a pipe through which smoke goes up into the air, usually through the roof of a building.

yell [jel] v. 소리치다, 고함치다; n. 고함소리, 부르짖음
If you yell, you shout loudly, usually because you are excited, angry, or in pain.

horrible [hɔ́ːrəbəl] a. 끔찍한, 소름 끼치게 싫은; 무서운
You can call something horrible when it causes you to feel great shock, fear, and disgust.

trick [trik] v. 속이다, 속임수를 쓰다; n. 속임수; (골탕을 먹이기 위한) 장난
If someone tricks you, they deceive you, often in order to make you do something.

Chapter 9

1. **How did Arthur feel when he woke up from the nightmare?**

   A. He felt that he would help his father with his cooking.

   B. He felt that even summer school was better than worrying.

   C. He felt that the envelope had to be thrown away for good.

   D. He felt that he had to keep the envelope a secret from his mother.

2. **What did Arthur make his mother promise before he showed her the envelope?**

   A. He made her promise that she would not get mad.

   B. He made her promise to explain the situation to Mr. Haney.

   C. He made her promise to help him avoid summer school.

   D. He made her promise to show him what was inside the envelope.

3. **What was really in the envelope?**

   A. Arthur's report card

   B. Arthur's history test

   C. Mr. Haney's tax documents

   D. Mr. Haney's party invitation

4. **What did Arthur's mother say regarding if it had been about Arthur?**

   A. She told him that he would be in big trouble.

   B. She told him that they would need to know.

   C. She told him that they would talk to Arthur's teachers.

   D. She told him that she would have wanted Arthur to keep it secret.

5. **Why did Arthur hurry out the door from his mother?**

   A. She was beginning to say that Arthur could be in trouble.

   B. She was beginning to ask Arthur to help her with math.

   C. Arthur was finally relieved to stop worrying about the envelope.

   D. Arthur wanted to tell D.W. that he was not in trouble after all.

1분에 몇 단어를 읽는지 리딩 속도를 측정해보세요.

$$\frac{529 \text{ words}}{\text{reading time (} \quad \text{) sec}} \times 60 = (\quad) \text{ WPM}$$

Build Your Vocabulary

cross [krɔːs] v. (서로) 교차하다, 엇갈리다; (가로질러) 건너다; n. X표, 십자가

If you cross your arms, legs, or fingers, you put one of them on top of the other.

mutter [mʌ́tər] v. 중얼거리다, 불평하다; n. 중얼거림, 불평

If you mutter, you speak very quietly so that you cannot easily be heard, often because you are complaining about something.

downstairs [dáunstέərz] ad. 아래층으로, 아래층에서; n. 아래층

If you go downstairs in a building, you go down a staircase toward the ground floor.

seasoning [síːzəniŋ] n. 양념

Seasoning is salt, pepper, or other spices that are added to food to improve its flavor.

worth [wəːrθ] a. ~의 가치가 있는; n. 가치, 값어치

If something is worth a particular action, or if an action is worth doing, it is considered to be important enough for that action.

lead [led] ① n. [광물] 납 ② v. 이끌다, 인솔하다; n. 선도, 지휘

Lead is a soft, gray, heavy metal.

envelope [énvəlòup] n. 봉투

An envelope is the rectangular paper cover in which you send a letter to someone through the post.

^{복습} **wastebasket** [wéistbæskit] n. 휴지통

A wastebasket is a container for rubbish, especially paper, which is usually placed on the floor in the corner of a room or next to a desk.

^{복습} **breath** [breθ] n. 숨, 호흡

Your breath is the air that you let out through your mouth when you breathe.

^{복습} **bother** [báðər] v. 신경 쓰이게 하다, 괴롭히다; 신경 쓰다, 애를 쓰다; n. 성가심

If something bothers you, or if you bother about it, it worries, annoys, or upsets you.

get something over with idiom (불쾌하지만 해야 할 일을) 끝내다, 완료하다

If you get something over with, you finish or complete something, usually you've tried to avoid because it's difficult or unpleasant to do.

be supposed to ~ idiom (관습·법·의무로) ~하기로 되어 있다

If you are supposed to do something, you are expected or required to do something according to a rule, a custom or an arrangement.

right away idiom 곧바로, 즉시

If you do something right away, you do it immediately.

^{복습} **nod** [nad] v. (고개를) 끄덕이다, 끄덕여 나타내다; n. (고개를) 끄덕임

If you nod, you move your head downward and upward to show agreement, understanding, or approval.

★ **slit** [slit] v. (slit-slit) (좁고) 길게 자르다; n. (좁고 기다란) 구멍

If you slit something, you make a long narrow cut in it.

^{복습} **glance** [glæns] v. 흘낏 보다, 잠깐 보다; n. 흘낏 봄

If you glance at something or someone, you look at them very quickly and then look away again immediately.

^{복습} **frown** [fraun] v. 얼굴[눈살]을 찌푸리다; n. 찡그림, 찌푸림

When someone frowns, their eyebrows become drawn together, because they are annoyed or puzzled.

exact [igzǽkt] a. 정확한, 정밀한 (exactly ad. 정확하게, 꼭)
Exact means correct in every detail.

frustrate [frʌ́streit] v. 좌절시키다, 불만스럽게 만들다; 방해하다
(frustrated a. 당혹스러운, 실망한, 좌절한)
If something frustrates you, it upsets or angers you because you are
unable to do anything about the problems it creates.

tax [tæks] n. 세금; v. 세금을 부과하다, 과세하다
Tax is an amount of money that you have to pay to the government so
that it can pay for public services.

document [dákjumənt] n. 서류, 문서
A document is one or more official pieces of paper with writing on them.

have nothing to do with ~ idiom ~와 관계가 없다
If you have nothing to do with someone or something, you do not have
connection with them.

murmur [mə́rməːr] v. 중얼거리다, 속삭이다; 투덜거리다; n. 중얼거림
If you murmur something, you say it very quietly, so that not many
people can hear what you are saying.

sigh [sai] v. 한숨 쉬다; n. 한숨, 탄식
When you sigh, you let out a deep breath, as a way of expressing feelings
such as disappointment, tiredness, or pleasure.

put off idiom (시간·날짜를) 미루다, 연기하다
If you put something off, you postpone or delay it.

torture [tɔ́ːrʧər] v. 고문하다; n. 고문
To torture someone means to cause them to suffer mental pain or
anxiety.

cheer [ʧiər] v. 응원하다, 환호성을 지르다; n. 환호(성)
If you are cheered by something, it makes you happier or less worried.

arrange [əréindʒ] v. (~하는 것을) 정하다, 마련하다; 배열하다, 정돈하다
If you arrange an event or meeting, you make plans for it to happen.

72

★ **hurried** [hə́:rid] a. 서둘러 하는 (hurriedly ad. 황급히, 다급하게)
A hurried action is done quickly, because you do not have much time
to do it in.

★ **bolt** [boult] v. 달아나다, 뛰기 시작하다; 빗장을 지르다; n. 빗장; 볼트
If a person or animal bolts, they suddenly start to run very fast, often
because something has frightened them.

Chapter 10

1. **Why did Arthur not call his friends immediately?**

   A. He was too tired to call them.

   B. It was not interesting news.

   C. He did not have their numbers.

   D. It was too late to call them.

2. **What did Arthur imagine Buster's reaction would be?**

   A. Arthur imagined that Buster would be disappointed.

   B. Arthur imagined that Buster would be pleased.

   C. Arthur imagined that Buster would be upset.

   D. Arthur imagined that Buster would be calm.

3. How did Arthur describe D.W.'s ideas?

A. He called them strange.

B. He called them dumb.

C. He called them crazy.

D. He called them funny.

4. Which of the following was NOT related to a question that D.W. asked Arthur?

A. She asked if Arthur was grounded for a year.

B. She asked if Arthur was moving to the garage.

C. She asked if Arthur was going to jail.

D. She asked if Arthur was going to a new school.

5. What did Arthur tell D.W. she would have to do in the end?

A. She would have to solve this mystery on her own.

B. She would have to think hard about it after sleeping.

C. She would have to ask their mother about the envelope later.

D. She would have to do something nice for Arthur before he told her.

1분에 몇 단어를 읽는지 리딩 속도를 측정해보세요.

$$\frac{243 \ words}{reading \ time \ (\quad) \ sec} \times 60 = (\quad) \ WPM$$

Build Your Vocabulary

⁑ **reaction** [riǽkʃən] n. 반응; 반작용
Your reaction to something that has happened or something that you
have experienced is what you feel, say, or do because of it.

way to go idiom 잘했어
People say 'way to go!' to encourage someone to continue the good
work.

⁑ **please** [pliːz] v. 기쁘게 하다, 즐겁게 하다 (pleased a. 기뻐하는, 만족해 하는)
If you are pleased, you are happy about something or satisfied with
something.

off the hook idiom 궁지를 벗어나다, 곤란에서 해방되다
If you are off the hook, you have escaped from a difficult situation.

⁑ **ground** [graund] v. (자녀에 대한 벌로) 외출하지 못하게 하다; n. 땅바닥, 지면
When parents ground a child, they forbid them to go out and enjoy
themselves for a period of time, as a punishment.

⁎ **jail** [dʒeil] n. 교도소, 감옥
A jail is a place where criminals are kept in order to punish them, or
where people waiting to be tried are kept.

복습 **stare** [stɛər] v. 응시하다, 뚫어지게 보다
If you stare at someone or something, you look at them for a long time.

shrug [ʃrʌg] v. (어깨를) 으쓱하다; n. (양 손바닥을 내보이면서 어깨를) 으쓱하기

If you shrug, you raise your shoulders to show that you are not interested in something or that you do not know or care about something.

disappoint [dìsəpɔ́int] v. 실망시키다, 낙담시키다

If things or people disappoint you, they are not as good as you had hoped, or do not do what you hoped they would do.

freeze [fri:z] v. (froze–frozen) (두려움 등으로 몸이) 얼어붙다; 얼다, 얼리다

If someone who is moving freezes, they suddenly stop and become completely still and quiet.

terror [térər] n. (극심한) 두려움, 무서움, 공포(심)

Terror is very great fear.

jumpy [dʒʌ́mpi] a. (놀람·공포로) 흠칫하는, 뛰어오르는, 조마조마한

If you are jumpy, you are nervous or worried about something.

frog [frɔ:g] n. 개구리

A frog is a small creature with smooth skin, big eyes, and long back legs which it uses for jumping.

imagination [imædʒənéiʃən] n. 상상력, 상상

Your imagination is the ability that you have to form pictures or ideas in your mind of things that are new and exciting, or things that you have not experienced.

come on idiom 자, 어서, 그러지 말고

People say 'come on' to encourage someone to do something.

garage [gərá:dʒ] n. 차고, 주차장

A garage is a building in which you keep a car.

make a face idiom 얼굴을 찌푸리다, 침울한 표정을 짓다

If you make a face, you twist your face to indicate a certain mental or emotional state.

1장

page 5

레이크우드 초등학교의 식당은 점심을 먹는 아이들로 가득 차 있었습니다. 몇몇은 집에서 샌드위치를 가져왔고, 나머지는 학교 급식을 먹고 있었습니다. 오늘의 메뉴는 그레이비 소스에 덮인 불가사의한 고기였습니다.

선생님 몇몇이 소음을 통제하려고 테이블 사이를 돌아다녔습니다.

"좀 조용히 하자." 랫번 선생님이 말했습니다. 그는 고개를 절레절레 흔들었습니다. "아무도 듣고 있지 않는 것 같네요."

page 6

스위트워터 선생님이 끄덕였습니다. "아니면 우리 말이 아예 들리지 않나보죠." 그녀가 말했습니다.

중앙에 있는 테이블 중 한 곳에서 아서와 그의 친구들은 다 먹어가고 있었습니다.

아서는 포크로 그의 음식을 찍었습니다. "그레이비가 없어도," 그는 말했습니다. "도대체 이게 어디서 온 음식인지 우리는 전혀 모를 거야."

"준비 됐니, 얘들아?" 프랜신이 물었습니다.

"준비 완료." 아서가 말했습니다. 그는 그의 쟁반을 옆으로 치웠습니다.

"기다리고 있어." 버스터가 말했습니다.

그들은 우유 하키 게임을 시작했습니다. 프랜신과 수 엘렌이 한 팀을 이루었습니다. 아서와 버스터가 다른 팀을 이루었습니다. 그들은 찌그러진 우유갑을 퍽으로 쓰며, 그것을 테이블 길이만큼 왔다 갔다 쳤습니다.

프랜신이 왼쪽으로 몸을 휙 움직이며 우유갑을 아서의 손 너머로 튕겨 보냈습니다. 버스터가 그것을 멈추려고 했지만, 퍽은 그를 지나 테이블 밖으로 미끄러졌습니다.

page 7

"골!" 머피가 말했습니다. 그녀가 공식적인 심판이었습니다.

프랜신이 미소 지었습니다. "그렇게 오래 걸리지 않았네." 그녀가 말했습니다.

아서는 손을 풀었습니다. "우리는 몸을 푸는 데 시간이 좀 걸릴 뿐이야."

"좋아." 수 엘렌이 말했습니다. "너희 몸이 따끈하게 다 풀리면 말해 줘."

"아마 우리 교체 선수가 필요할 거야." 버스터가 말했습니다. 그는 빙키 반스 쪽으로 몸을 돌렸습니다. "너 차례로 할래?"

"아니." 주먹으로 다른 우유갑을 찌그러뜨리며 빙키가 말했습니다. 그는 단지 퍽을 만드는 것을 좋아할 뿐이었습니다.

"주목해 주세요!"

학교 비서인 팅글리 씨가 스피커를

통해 말하고 있었습니다.

"아서 리드, *지금 당장* 하니 교장 선생님 사무실로 오세요."

정적이 식당 안을 덮었습니다. 모두 아서를 쳐다보았습니다. 버스터의 입은 활짝 열렸고, 빙키의 손은 찌그러뜨리다 말고 멈췄습니다.

"이런!" 프랜신이 말했습니다.

"내 말이." 머피가 말했습니다.

수 엘렌은 그저 고개를 저을 뿐이었습니다.

"너 정말 큰일 났다, 아서." 버스터가 말했습니다. 때때로 하니 교장 선생님은 버스터가 복도에서 뛰어다닌다고 소리를 질렀습니다. 하지만 그가 *교장실*에 불려간 적은 딱 한 번, 랫번 선생님 책상 위에 재채기 가루를 올려놓았을 때밖에 없었습니다.

"너 괜찮니, 아서?" 프랜신이 물었습니다.

"그, 그런 것 같아."

"전혀 괜찮아 보이지 않아." 수 엘렌이 말했습니다. "책에서 읽을 수 있는 사슴 같아 보이는데. 차 헤드라이트를 쳐다보는 그 사슴 있잖아."

"충격받은 것 같아." 빙키가 말했습니다. "아서는 교장실에 가는 게 익숙하지 않아. 나는 눈을 가리고 한 팔이 등 뒤로 묶인 채로도 갈 수 있는데."

"너 무슨 일을 한 거니, 아서?" 프랜신이 물었습니다.

아서는 고개를 저었습니다. "모르겠어. 생각나는 게 아무것도 없어."

빙키가 코웃음을 쳤습니다. "하니 교장 선생님한테 그 변명을 써먹으려고 하지 마. 내 경우에는 절대 안 먹혔어."

아서는 일어섰습니다. "응, 나 이제 가야할 것 같아."

"아서, 널 알게 되어 기뻤어." 프랜신이 말했습니다.

"행운을 빌어." 버스터가 말했습니다. "그리고 너 그 감자를 다 안 먹을 거면..." 그는 아서의 접시를 가리켰습니다.

아서는 그의 쟁반을 건네 밀었습니다. "마음껏 먹어." 그는 말했습니다. "난 방금 식욕을 잃었어."

2장

아서가 교실로 돌아왔을 때, 그의 친구들이 그에게 달려 왔습니다.

"너 살아남았구나!" 버스터가 말했습니다.

"고문을 받은 또렷한 흔적 없이." 빙키가 덧붙였습니다. 그는 조금 실망한 듯이 보였습니다.

"무슨 일이 있었니?" 프랜신이 물었습니다.

아서는 한숨을 쉬었습니다. "하니 교장 선생님이 이것을 주셨어." 그는 큰 갈색 봉투를 들었습니다. "엄마한테 전하라고 하셨어."

"그게 다야?" 머피가 물었습니다. 그녀는 가까이 보기 위해 다가섰습니다. "뭐라고 적혀 있니? 밀봉되어 있어?"

page 12

프랜신이 봉투를 잡았습니다. "밀봉되어 있군, 좋아." 그녀는 그것을 빛 쪽으로 들어 올렸습니다. "그리고 안을 비춰 보기엔 너무 두꺼워."

"흔들어 봐." 버스터가 귀를 쫑긋 세우며 말했습니다.

프랜신은 잠시 동안 봉투를 흔들었습니다. 그것은 부드럽게 바스락거렸습니다. "그다지 도움이 되지 않는데." 그녀가 말했습니다.

빙키가 팔짱을 끼면서 말했습니다. "그냥 열어 보자."

"그럴 수 없어." 아서가 말했습니다. "이건 우리 엄마 앞으로 보내진 거야. 그리고 뭐라고 찍혀 있는지 봐. '개인적인' 그리고 '기밀의'."

"별로 안 좋은 신호인데." 버스터가 말했습니다. "좋은 소식은 절대 개인적이지 않아."

"게다가," 빙키가 말했습니다. "네가

어떤 문제에 닥친 건지 알 때까지 변명할 거리를 미리 만들 수도 없잖아."

"하니 교장 선생님이 아무런 단서를 주지 않았니?" 프랜신이 물었습니다.

"중요하다고 하셨어." 봉투를 다시 가져가며 아서가 말했습니다. "그게 전부였어."

page 13

"만약 그게 좋은 소식이라면," 머피가 말했습니다. "하니 교장 선생님께서 말해 줬을 거야. 우리 엄마는 새로운 리무진을 사거나 요리사가 저녁식사에 특별 디저트를 만들면 항상 바로 말해 주거든."

"교장 선생님은 전혀 그런 식으로 말하지 않았어." 아서가 인정했습니다.

"그건 나쁜 소식이라는 뜻이지." 프랜신이 말했습니다. "문제는, 얼마나 나쁘냐는 거야."

이것은 아서가 생각하고 싶은 질문이 아니었습니다.

빙키가 웃었습니다. "오 맞아! 너 도서관 책을 잃어버린 것이 틀림없어."

"하니 교장 선생님이 연체된 도서관 책에 관여하실 거라고 생각하지 않아." 아서가 말했습니다. "게다가, 나 방금 다 반납했는걸."

"오, 안 돼!" 프랜신이 말했습니다.

"뭔데 그래?" 머피가 말했습니다.

"우리에게 말해 봐." 버스터가 말했습

니다.

page 14

"나한테 말해 줘!" 아서가 말했습니다.

"아무것도 아니야." 프랜신이 말했습니다. "생각하기에 너무 끔찍해서."

아서는 창백해졌습니다. "그러니까 나한테 말해 줘야지."

"좋아." 프랜신이 말했습니다. "하지만 네가 말하라고 강요한 거야." 그녀는 몸서리쳤습니다. "만약 네가 랫번 선생님의 역사 시험을 통과하지 못한 것이라면?"

아서는 얼굴을 찌푸렸습니다. 그 중요한 시험은 지난주에 있었습니다. 그것은 어려운 시험이었습니다.

"기억나, 아서? 너 선교사들이 어떻게 1620년에 아메리카 대륙에 오게 됐는지 적었다고 말했잖아."

"프랜신, 선교사들은 정말로 1620년에 왔어."

그녀는 놀란 것처럼 보였습니다. "진짜야?"

모두들 고개를 끄덕거렸습니다.

"뭐, 아무튼…" 프랜신은 봉투를 두드렸습니다. "증거는 바로 여기 있어. 그리고 만약 네가 낙제했다면, 넌 아마도 1년 전체를 낙제한 것일 수도 있어. 너는 그게 무슨 뜻인지 알 거야. 서머스쿨(여름 보충 수업)."

page 15

아서는 의자에 앉아 그의 운명에 대해 생각했습니다. 서머스쿨. 아마도 영어에서 가장 무서운 두 단어.

그는 어두운 지하 감옥의 벽에 사슬로 묶여 있는 자신을 보았습니다. 창살 밖으로, 그는 그의 친구들이 노는 것을 들을 수 있었습니다. 그는 창살 사이로 바라보았습니다. 버스터와 브레인은 캠핑을 위해 텐트를 치고 있었습니다. 머피와 프루넬라는 롤러 블레이드를 타고 있었습니다.

아서는 자신의 감옥 안을 둘러보았습니다. 그는 오로지 두껍고, 먼지투성이인 책만을 동무 삼아 혼자 있었습니다. 그리고 감시인 랫번 선생님이 걸어 들어왔습니다. 그는 아이스크림콘을 후루룩 소리 내며 먹었습니다. 아이스크림 몇 방울이 아서가 닿지 않는 바닥에 떨어졌습니다.

"정신 좀 차려, 아서!" 버스터가 말했습니다.

아서는 그의 친구들을 멍하니 쳐다봤습니다.

page 17

"너 사람들이 하는 말 알잖아." 버스터가 계속 말했습니다. "역사를 배우지 않는 사람은 그 역사를 반복할 불운을 피할 수 없다고."

아서는 한숨 쉬었습니다. 역사이건

아니건, 그는 확실히 불운한 기분이었
습니다.

3장

page 18

아서는 학교가 끝난 후 봉투를 곧장
집으로 가져갈 수도 있었습니다. 하지만
그는 그러지 않았습니다.

"하니 교장 선생님은 정확히 언제 봉
투를 전해야 하는지 말씀하진 않으셨
어." 브레인이 그에게 말했었습니다. "국
제법상 너는 계획을 세울 권리가 있어."

그들은 슈가 볼의 칸막이 자리에 앉
아 있었습니다. 버스터와 프랜신도 그곳
에 있었습니다. 프루넬라와 머피는 그들
뒤에 앉아 있었습니다.

아서는 사탕을 조금 사왔지만, 먹고
있지는 않았습니다. 그는 단지 그것을
자기 앞에서 이리저리 옮길 뿐이었습니
다. 사탕은 큰 물음표가 있는 직사각형
모양으로 놓여졌습니다.

page 19

브레인은 아서의 봉투를 유심히 쳐다
보았습니다. "만약에 내가 엑스레이 투
시력이 있다면..." 그가 말했습니다.

버스터가 그에게서 봉투를 잡았습니
다. "우리 행동으로 옮겨야 해! 나는 너
없이 재미있는 일들을 하면서 여름을

보내고 싶지 않아." 그는 봉투를 테이블
끝으로 밀었습니다. "이봐, 만약에 네가
봉투를 우연히 잃어버린다면 어떻게 될
까?"

그는 봉투를 바닥으로 밀쳤습니다.

"이건 쓰레기통으로 버려질 수도 있
어. 분쇄기로 갈 수도 있고. 그리고 나
서 불도저에 밀려 쓰레기 매립지로 가겠
지. 오로지 갈매기들만이 그곳에서 이
것을 읽을 거야. 그리고 우리는 갈매기
들이 어떻게 생각할지 걱정하지 않아도
돼."

"그건 맞아." 아서가 말했습니다.

프루넬라가 봉투를 집어 들었습니다.

"그의 말을 듣지 마, 아서. 그는 앞날
을 내다보고 있지 않아. 너는 마지막에
비난받지 않을 방법을 생각해야 해." 그
녀는 잠시 멈추었습니다. "아마 너는 그
걸 세탁 바구니에 숨길 수 있을 거야.
그리고 그게 *씻겨나가는 거지*." 그녀는
봉투가 마치 젖어서 물이 뚝뚝 떨어지
는 것처럼 조심스럽게 들어 올렸습니다.
"너희 엄마는 읽을 수 없을 테지만, 넌
비난받지 않을 거야."

page 20

"세탁." 아서가 말했습니다. "흥미로운
데."

"흥미롭지 않아." 머피가 말했습니다.
"위험해. 넌 그걸 집에서 가능한 멀리 보
내 버려야 해. 알래스카나 팀북투로 가

는 1등석 티켓을 사서 그걸 보내 버려.”

“난 그럴 만한 돈이 없어.” 아서가 말했습니다.

그는 시계를 쳐다보았습니다. 집으로 가야 할 시간이었습니다.

모두들 밖으로 나왔습니다.

프랜신은 여전히 얼굴을 찌푸리고 있었습니다. “벗어날 방법이 분명 있을 거야.” 그녀가 말했습니다.

브레인은 배수구 아래로 내다보았습니다. “여기에 떨어뜨리면 되겠다.” 그가 말했습니다. “물살이 그걸 베어 호수로 데려갈 거고, 그리고 거기서부터 오터 강으로 흘러갈 거야. 그게 항구에 도착하고 나면, 다시 바다로 쓸려가겠지. 어쩌면 유럽까지 말이야. 그게 마침내 해안가로 밀려 올라왔을 때, 어떤 엄마가 그것을 발견할 수도 있어. 하지만 그녀는 아마 영어를 이해하지 못할 거고, 그럼 넌 안전하겠지.”

“유럽은 아주 멀어.” 아서가 말했습니다.

프랜신은 브레인의 손에서 봉투를 잡아챘습니다. “그러지 마, 아서.” 그녀는 말했습니다. “만약 네가 이것을 잃어버리려고 한다면, 넌 이중으로 문제에 처할 거야. 잃어버린 것에 대해서, 그리고 그게 무엇이든 네가 애초에 했던 일에 대해서.”

그녀는 봉투를 그에게 돌려주었습니다.

“모든 것이 공평하지 않아.” 아서가 말했습니다. “나는 아무것도 하지 않았다고! 나는 그냥 이 봉투를 엄마에게 갖다드리고 무슨 일이 일어나는지 지켜볼 거야.”

그는 그렇게 말하는 것이 그의 기분을 나아지게 해주길 바랐었지만, 그렇게 되지 않았습니다.

“그건 마지막 방법이야.” 브레인이 말했습니다. “하지만 물론 선택권은 너에게 있어.”

4장

“다녀왔습니다!” 아서는 조심스럽게 외쳤습니다.

그의 강아지, 팔 이외에는 부엌에 아무도 없었습니다. 그래도 아서는 엄마가 집에 있다는 것을 알았습니다. 엄마 차가 차고 진입로에 있었습니다.

“그래도 엄마는 바쁠 거야.” 그가 팔에게 말했습니다. “사실, 난 그럴 거라 확신해. 엄마는 일하거나, D.W.를 도와주거나, 아기 케이트를 돌보고 있을 수도 있어. 난 엄마를 방해하고 싶지 않아.”

팔이 짖었습니다.

“너 배고프니?” 아서가 말했습니다.

팔은 꼬리를 흔들었습니다.

아서는 배낭을 조리대에 내려놓았습니다. 하니 교장 선생님이 주신 봉투의 한 모퉁이가 가방 덮개 밖으로 삐져나와 있었습니다. 그리고 그는 팔의 밥그릇을 씻기 시작했습니다.

page 25

“하니 교장 선생님께서 엄마한테 봉투를 드리라고 하셨어.” 아서는 팔에게 설명했습니다. “하지만 그 안에 무엇이 들어있는지는 말씀하지 않으셨지.”

팔이 짖었습니다.

“안 돼.” 아서가 말했습니다, “난 봉투를 먹을 수 없어.”

팔이 다시 짖었습니다.

“안 돼, 난 뒷마당에 묻을 수도 없어.”

그는 빈 그릇을 바닥에 내려놓았습니다. 팔은 실망하여 낑낑거렸습니다.

“친구들은 모두 틀림없이 나쁜 소식일 거라고 생각해.” 아서가 계속했습니다.

팔은 계속해서 낑낑거렸습니다.

“프랜신은 내가 랫번 선생님의 역사 시험을 낙제했을 거라고 생각해. 그녀는 내가 서머스쿨을 가야 할 거라고 말해.” 아서는 얼굴을 찡그렸습니다.

팔은 아서의 옆에서 위아래로 뛰었습니다.

아서는 식료품 창고에서 개 사료를 가져왔습니다. “어쩌면 이걸 그냥 꺼내놓

기만 하고 아무 말도 하지 않을까 싶어. 하니 교장 선생님은 내가 엄마에게 전하게 집으로 가져가라고 말했지, 내가 실제로 엄마한테 드려야 한다고는 말하지 않았어. 아마 엄마는 이걸 알아차리지도 못하실 거야.”

page 26

아서는 그릇을 테이블 위에 올려놓은 다음, 가방을 열었습니다. 그는 조심스레 봉투를 꺼내 테이블 위에 올렸습니다.

“그게 뭐야?”

아서가 휙 돌아보고는 그의 여동생 D.W.가 현관에 서 있는 것을 발견했습니다.

“뭐가 뭐야?”

D.W.가 가리켰습니다. “봉투 말이야, 멍청아.”

“아무것도 아니야!” 그가 소리쳤습니다. 그는 테이블에 기댔습니다. “이건 그냥 멍청한 오래된 봉투야. 사람들은 이 봉투를 몇 주 동안 지나치면서도 알아차리지 못할 거야. 그리고 만약 안다고 해도, 이런 따분한 봉투는 굳이 열어 보려고 하지 않겠지.”

“아무것도 아닌 것 치고는 뭔가 많은데.” D.W.가 말했습니다. “오빠 정말 이상하게 행동하고 있어.”

page 27

“나 이상하게 굴고 있지 않아.” 아서가 대답했습니다. 그는 곧게 서서 팔짱

을 꼈습니다. "난 걱정돼. 아니 그러니까 내 말은, 걱정되지 않아. 난 바빠. 그게 다야. 바빠. 3학년은 너무 바빠."

D.W.는 의자로 올라가서 아서의 눈을 쳐다보았습니다. "날 속이지 마." 그녀가 말했습니다. "난 오빠가 걱정하는 걸 보면 알아."

아서는 눈을 깜박였습니다. "정말?"

D.W.는 고개를 끄덕였습니다. "어. 오빠 주름 생기거든."

"내가 그래?"

그녀는 고개를 끄덕였습니다. "난 놀라지 않았어. 오빠는 많은 일에 대해 걱정할 수 있겠지. 예를 들면 언젠가 생일 선물을 받기에는 너무 나이가 들 것이라는 점. 또는 부기맨이 진짜로 있어서, 오빠가 침대 밑을 확인하는 것을 깜박하는 날을 기다리고 있다고 생각하고 있을 수도 있지."

page 29

아서는 한숨 쉬었습니다. "그것들은 일상적인 걱정이지. 매일의 걱정. 난 그것들은 감당할 수 있어."

D.W.는 아서를 주의 깊게 쳐다보았습니다. "그럼 더 있단 말이야? 자, 털어놓아 봐."

"알겠어, 알겠어!" 아서가 말했습니다. "교장 선생님이 엄마 드리라고 이 봉투를 주셨어. 그게 다야. 이제 날 좀 내버려 뒤!"

하지만 D.W.는 아직 끝나지 않았습니다. 그녀는 봉투를 한번 쳐다보았습니다. "이게 무슨 말이야?" 그녀가 물었습니다.

"무슨 말?"

"앞에 적혀 있는 이 큰 글자들."

"'개인적인' 그리고 '기밀의'."

D.W.는 얼굴을 찌푸렸습니다. "'개인적인'은 알아. '기—밀—의'는 무슨 뜻이야?"

아서는 한숨 쉬었습니다. "엄마만이 볼 수 있다는 뜻이야."

D.W.의 눈이 크게 떠졌습니다. 그녀는 의자에서 내려와 노래를 부르며 복도로 팔짝팔짝 뛰어갔습니다.

page 30

"아서 오빠는 큰일 났데요,
아서 오빠는 큰일 났데요."

이번만큼은, 아서는 그녀와 말다툼하지 않았습니다. 그는 그녀가 옳다는 것을 알고 있었습니다.

5장

page 31

좋은 소식은 D.W.가 갑자기 노래를 멈추었다는 것입니다. 나쁜 소식은 그녀가 엄마와 부딪혀서 노래를 멈추었다는 것입니다.

"천천히 움직이렴, 얘야. 우리는 집 안에 신호등을 달 수 없단다."

리드 부인은 D.W.에게 짧은 입맞춤을 했습니다. 그녀의 손은 서류들로 가득했습니다.

"정말 끔찍한 하루야! 만약 내가 두 개의 머리와 네 개의 손이 있어도, 나는 여전히 뒤쳐졌을 거야."

리드 부인은 회계사였습니다. 그녀는 세금 정산 시기가 되면 언제나 약간 지쳤습니다.

"엄마, 아서 오빠가 이상하게 행동해요. 집으로—"

"이봐!" 아서가 말했습니다. "그건 네가 상관할 바가—"

"조용히 하렴, 아서!" 엄마가 말했습니다. "D.W. 지금은 안 돼. 나는 전화를 몇 통 해야 한단다."

그녀는 서류들을 조리대에 올려놓았습니다.

"아서, 이게 뭐니?"

아서는 움찔했습니다. "그거요?"

"그래, 그거." 그녀는 봉투와 그 옆에 있는 팔의 밥그릇을 가리켰습니다. "테이블 위에."

"테이블이요? 여기요? 부엌 안에?"

엄마는 팔짱을 꼈습니다. "그래, 부엌 테이블. 언제부터 팔이 여기서 먹었지?"

아서는 깊은 한숨을 쉬었습니다.

"여기서 안 먹어요."

"그럼 왜 팔의 밥그릇을 테이블 위에 올려놓은 거니?" 그녀는 그것을 바닥에 내려놓았습니다. "아서, 솔직히 난 네가 더 조심하길 기대한단다."

아서가 꼼지락거리는 동안, 리드 부인은 전화기를 들고 번호를 눌렀습니다. 그녀는 비서에게 메시지를 남겼습니다.

"이게 오늘 오후에 벌써 세 번째로 전화한 거야. 이 사람은 절대 연락이 닿지 않아." 그녀는 아서를 쳐다보았습니다. "괜찮니? 너 좀 창백해 보이는구나."

"물론이죠." 아서가 말했습니다. "전 그냥 생각하고 있었어요. 음... 저녁 먹을 준비를 하는 걸요." 그는 서랍에서 포크와 나이프를 꺼내 각각의 식탁 의자 앞에 놓기 시작했습니다.

"우편이요!" 리드 씨가 편지 한 뭉치를 들고 오면서 말했습니다. 그는 그것들을 아서의 봉투 위에 놓았습니다.

"모두들 오늘 어땠어?"

"여보, 당신 귀 뒤에 휘핑크림이 묻어 있어요."

"정말? 나는 다 닦아냈다고 생각했는데." 그는 손가락으로 크림을 닦아냈습니다. "새로운 디저트를 실험 중이었거든."

리드씨는 그의 음식 출장 서비스 사업으로 매우 바빴습니다.

"아무도 다치지 않았기를 바라요." 리드 부인이 말했습니다.

리드 씨는 한숨 쉬었습니다. "오직 파이 껍질만이 살아남지 못했어."

전화가 울렸습니다.

"내가 받을게요." 리드 부인이 말했습니다. 그녀는 전화를 받으면서 우편물과 봉투를 들었습니다. "여보세요? 오, 안녕하세요, 리아."

그녀는 우편물을 훑어보기 시작했습니다.

편지 하나가 휴지통으로 들어갔습니다.

"아니, 아니에요. 당신한테 전화가 와서 실망한 게 아니에요. 허브 씨한테 연락이 오길 기다리고 있었거든요."

그녀는 나중을 위해 청구서를 옆으로 치워두었습니다.

page 36

"그한테 서류 받을 것이 있어요."

그녀는 잡지를 넘겨봤습니다.

"네, 알아요. 월요일이 마감이에요."

아서는 높아져가는 파멸의 기운을 느끼며 엄마를 바라보았습니다. 그는 문 쪽으로 조금씩 움직였습니다. 엄마가 하니 교장 선생님의 봉투에 닿아 있었습니다.

갑자기 가스레인지 위의 물이 끓어 넘치기 시작했습니다.

"오, 이만 가 봐야 해요." 리드 부인이 말했습니다. "나중에 이야기해요, 리아." 그녀는 전화를 끊고 봉투를 조리대 가장자리에 놓았습니다. 그녀는 가스레인지 쪽으로 몸을 돌렸습니다.

봉투가 불안정하게 잠깐 움직이더니, 이내 휴지통 안으로 떨어졌습니다.

아서는 안도감으로 털썩 주저앉았습니다. 그는 결백했습니다. 그가 봉투를 쓰레기통에 넣은 것이 아니었습니다. 어떤 다른 손이 그것을 그곳으로 인도했습니다. 그것은 필연이었습니다. 그것은 운명이었습니다. 그것은 처음부터 그렇게 될 예정이었습니다.

6장

page 37

저녁식사는 삼키기가 힘들었습니다. 어떻게 아서가 먹는 데에 집중할 수 있었겠어요? 그가 고개를 들 때마다, 그는 휴지통에서 봉투가 그를 쳐다보고 있는 것을 보았습니다.

그들이 햄버거와 감자튀김을 먹고 있다는 사실도 그를 기쁘게 하지 않았습니다. 그의 반쯤 먹은 햄버거는 초승달처럼 접시의 가장자리에 놓여 있었습니다. 보통 그는 감자튀김을 성벽처럼 쌓고, 초록깍지콩을 성 주위의 연못에 있는 악어처럼 늘어놓았습니다. 하지만 오늘밤엔 그는 단지 감자튀김과 콩을 포크로 내리찍을 뿐이었습니다. 그것들은 잘게 조각난 카펫처럼 보였습니다.

page 38

"너 지금 이빨이 닳는 것을 막으려고 하는 거니, 아서?" 엄마가 물었습니다.

아서는 혼란스러워 보였습니다.

그녀는 그의 접시를 가리켰습니다. "그렇게 으깨는 거. 너 그것들을 다 먹어야 하는 거 알지? 우리는 음식을 낭비하길 원하지 않는단다."

아서는 작은 한 입을 먹었습니다.

그의 아빠는 샐러드를 더 집어먹었습니다. "너 오늘 밤엔 몹시 조용하구나, 아서." 그가 말했습니다.

아서는 그의 의자에서 몸을 꼼지락거렸습니다. "오늘 학교에서 너무 열심히 했거든요." 그는 아빠를 쳐다보았습니다. "아빠가 학교 다닐 때, 시험이 중요했나요?"

"오, 그럼. 우리는 요즘 아이들이 하는 것처럼 그렇게 다양한 과제들은 없었어. 어떤 때에는 한 번의 시험이 전체 성적의 반을 차지하고는 했단다."

page 39

"그렇게 많이요?"

그의 아빠는 미소 지었습니다. "당연하지. 너희들이 학교생활을 쉽게 한다고 하지는 않을게. 하지만 너희들은 확실히 더 많은 선택을 가지고 있단다."

"가장 중요한 것은," 리드 부인이 말했습니다. "우리는 너희가 최선을 다하기를 바란단다."

"나는 언제나 최선을 다해요." 케이트와 감자튀김을 바꾸며 D.W.가 말했습니다. "다 내 계획의 일부에요."

"무슨 계획 말이니, 아가야?" 엄마가 물었습니다.

"세계 지배를 하는 계획이요." 아서가 말했습니다.

"아서!" 아빠가 말했습니다.

"죄송해요." 아서가 주제를 바꿨습니다. "아빠는 학교생활의 모든 부분이 중요하다고 생각하세요? 그러니까, 어떤 것들은 다른 것들보다 더 중요하지 않나요?"

리드 씨는 고개를 저었습니다. "뭐라고 말하기 어렵구나. 네 나이 때, 나는 음식 출장 서비스 사업을 할 거라고 전혀 계획하지 않았어. 그리고 내 일이 음식과 관련된 것이지만, 나는 여전히 계획을 세우기 위해서는 수학을, 그리고 광고를 위해서는 어떻게 글을 쓰는지를 알 필요가 있단다."

page 40

"그러면, 어, 역사는 어때요?" 아서가 말했습니다. "그건 그렇게 중요하지 않겠죠? 그렇죠?"

"역사 역시 중요하단다." 아빠가 말했습니다. "내가 오래된 조리법을 공부하거나 역사적인 주제를 가지고 식사를 만들 수도 있잖니."

"알겠어요." 아서는 그렇지 않길 바라면서 말했습니다.

"모든 것에 대해서 배우는 건 타당하단다." 엄마가 말했습니다. "너는 나중에 언제 그것이 도움이 될지 알 수 없어." 그녀는 테이블 저편을 내려다보았습니다. "아서, 감자튀김 좀 전해주렴."

아서는 그릇을 들었습니다.

D.W.는 미소 지었습니다. "아서 오빠, 말 나온 김에 엄마한테 주고 싶은 다른 무언가가 있지 않아?"

아서는 테이블 밑에서 D.W.를 발로 차고 싶은 것을 간신히 참았습니다. "그냥 저의 감사요." 그는 말했습니다. "맛있는 저녁을 만들어 주신 것에 대한."

page 42

그는 으깬 감자튀김과 콩을 포크로 들어 입을 채웠습니다.

엄마는 그를 쳐다보았습니다. "고맙다, 아서—그렇구나."

그녀가 무언가 더 말할 수도 있었지만, 전화가 울렸습니다. 그녀는 전화를 받으려고 벌떡 일어났습니다.

벨소리 덕에 살았다고 아서는 생각했습니다. 적어도 지금은 말이지요.

7장

page 43

저녁식사 후, 아서는 숙제를 하러 방으로 갔습니다.

rope와 hope와 운율이 맞는 단어를 생각하시오.

"으아아아!" 아서가 소리냈습니다.

그는 재빨리 수학으로 바꿨습니다. 첫 번째 문제는 직사각형을 반으로 자르는 것에 대한 것이었습니다.

"내가 그 봉투를 반으로 자를 수 있으면 좋겠네." 아서가 말했습니다.

다른 문제는 편지로 가득 찬 우편주머니에 관한 것이었습니다. 봉투에 대한 언급은 없었지만, 아서가 생각할 수 있는 것은 온통 봉투밖에 없었습니다.

page 44

그는 종이 가장자리에 끄적거리기 시작했습니다. 그는 큰 직사각형, 거대한 직사각형, 세상에서 가장 큰 직사각형을 그리기 시작했습니다.

하지만 그것이 단지 직사각형이었을까요? 아니, 그것은 거대한 봉투였습니다. 그리고 그것은 아서를 언덕 아래로 쫓아가고 있었습니다. 그것은 빙글빙글 회전하면서 굴렀습니다. 아서는 가까스로 앞서 갔습니다.

"도망가지 마." 봉투가 말하고 있었습니다. "난 네가 내 안에 딱 들어맞을 것이라는 걸 알아. 그리고 걱정하지 마. 난 널 절대 나가게 하지 않을게."

"아니야, 사양할게." 아서가 말했습니다. "난 납작해질 거야." 그는 더 빨리 뛰었습니다.

"그건 내 잘못이 아니야." 봉투가 숨을 헐떡이며 말했습니다. "난 단지 좋은 체형이 아닐 뿐이야."

아서는 눈을 비볐습니다. 그는 휴식이 필요했습니다.

그는 케이트의 방을 살짝 보았습니다. 그녀는 이미 잠들었습니다.

page 45

"아기들은 운이 좋아." 그는 중얼거렸습니다. "그들은 봉투에 대해 걱정하지 않아도 돼. 아니면 역사 시험이나. 아니면 서머스쿨에 대해서. 그들은 단지 귀여워 보이고 기저귀를 가득 채우기만 하면 돼."

케이트는 자면서 몸을 돌렸고, 담요가 그녀에게서 미끄러졌습니다.

아서는 담요를 다시 덮어 주었습니다. "좋았던 옛 시절이여." 그는 한숨 쉬었습니다.

그의 엄마는 사무실에 앉아 있었습니다. 그녀는 일하면서 연필을 깨물고 노래를 흥얼거리고 있었습니다. 아서는 발끝으로 조심조심 걸으며 문을 지나갔습니다. 그는 아빠와 D.W.가 TV에서 고양이 노래방 쇼를 보고 있는 것을 발견했습니다.

고양이들은 노래 부르면서 밀짚모자를 쓰고 줄을 맞춰 춤을 추고 있었습니다.

"저 고양이들은 정말 미쳤어요." D.W.가 말했습니다. "이제 잘 보세요. 여기가 제일 재미있는 부분이에요."

"네가 어떻게 아니?" 아빠가 물었습니다.

page 47

아서가 앉았습니다. "얘는 이 에피소드를 84번 봤어요." 그가 설명했습니다.

"그리고 볼 때마다 더 재미있어져." D.W.가 말했습니다. 그녀는 음악에 맞춰 머리를 흔들었습니다.

그녀의 아빠도 같이 흥얼거렸습니다. "모든 고양이가 저렇게 춤출 수 있는 것이 아니야." 그가 지적했습니다. "그건 많은 연습이 필요하지."

광고가 시작되었습니다.

"일상의 스트레스가 당신을 우울하게 만드나요?"

아서가 끄덕였습니다.

"당신이 더 이상 통제가 되지 않는다고 느껴지나요?"

아서는 다시 끄덕였습니다.

"지끈거림, 지끈거림. 그것은 절대 멈추지 않습니다."

아서는 그의 머리를 팔로 감쌌습니다. "예전의 당신 자신처럼 다시 느끼기 위해서, 페인프리나 페인프리 플러스를

써 보세요. 두통이 몇 분 안에 사라집니다."

아서는 일어섰습니다. 그가 문제를 해결하기 위한 약을 먹을 수 있다면 좋을 텐데. 하지만 문제는 그렇게 간단하지 않았습니다.

"너 정말 피곤해 보이는구나, 아서." 그의 아빠가 말했습니다.

"네 그래요." 아서가 인정했습니다.

"쉿!" D.W.가 말했습니다. "고양이들이 이제 '털뭉치'를 노래할 거예요. 난 그 노래를 좋아해요."

아서는 그것을 듣기 위해 남아 있지 않았습니다. 조용한 "안녕히 주무세요." 인사와 함께, 그는 잠자러 침대로 올라갔습니다.

8장

아서가 잠잘 준비가 되었을 때, 베개를 바라보고 있는 자신을 발견했습니다. 그 이전까지 아서는 베개가 속이 꽉 찬 봉투와 얼마나 닮았는지 알아차리지 못했었습니다.

양치질을 하면서, 아서는 그의 얼굴을 거울 바로 앞으로 가져갔습니다. 그의 이빨은 작은 사각형으로 줄지어 있었습니다.

거의 봉투와 같네, 라고 그는 생각했습니다.

그가 보는 모든 곳에서, 즉 벽지, 카펫, 담요에 있는 무늬에서 그는 봉투를 보았습니다. 그것들은 다양한 형태와 크기를 가지고 있었습니다.

"봉투가 머릿속에서 떠나질 않아." 그는 결론 내렸습니다. "나한테 지금 필요한 것은 푹 자는 거야."

아서는 침대 위에 올라가 이불을 덮었습니다.

"아직 깨어 있어, 아서 오빠?" D.W.가 문가에 서 있었습니다.

"아니, 난 완전히 잠들었어. 넌 나쁜 꿈이야. 가 버려."

"만약 오빠가 완전히 잠들었다면, 어떻게 나한테 가 버리라고 말할 수 있지?"

아서는 일어났습니다. "원하는 게 뭐야?"

"난 오빠가 어떤 사고를 쳤는지 알고 싶어."

"아무런 문제 없어, D.W."

그녀는 납득하지 않았습니다. "그 신비로운 봉투 안에 뭐가 있었어?"

"나도 몰라." 아서는 정직하게 말했습니다.

"엄마가 아무 말도 하지 않았어?"

"어, 아무 말씀 없었어."

"오." D.W.는 실망했습니다. "걱정하지 마. 난 오빠가 다른 사고를 칠 거라고 확신해."

page 51

"고마워, D.W. 그 말이 나를 훨씬 기분 좋게 해주는구나."

"언제든지." D.W.가 말하고는 방으로 돌아갔습니다.

아서는 천장을 바라보았습니다. 엄밀히 말하면, 그는 D.W.에게 사실을 말한 것이었습니다. 엄마는 그에게 봉투에 무엇이 들어있는지 말하지 않았었습니다. 물론, 그것은 그녀가 봉투를 아직 보지 않았기 때문이지요. 봉투는 여전히 휴지통 안에 놓여 있었습니다.

왜 그게 거기 그냥 있으면 안 되는 건데?, 라고 아서는 생각했습니다.

그는 아주 잠깐인 듯한 순간 동안 눈을 감았습니다.

그의 눈이 떠졌습니다.

아서는 종이가 바스락거리는 소리를 들었습니다. 무엇이 소리를 내는 거지? 그는 침대에서 나와 귀를 기울였습니다.

소리는 아래층에서 나고 있었습니다.

page 52

아서는 소음을 따라 부엌으로 들어갔습니다. 휴지통이 흔들리고 있었는데, 마치 무언가가 그 안에서 이리저리 튀고 있는 것 같았습니다. 아서는 아래를 바라보았습니다. 하니 교장 선생님께서 주신 봉투가 바로 그의 눈앞에서 점점 커지고 있었습니다! 휴지통은 더 이상 그걸 담아두지 못했습니다.

아서는 봉투를 꺼내서 위층으로 달려갔습니다. 봉투가 그의 팔에서 퍼덕거렸습니다. 그것은 옮기기에 너무 커지고 있었습니다. 아서는 바닥을 따라 그것을 끌면서 화장실로 갔습니다. 그는 욕조로 그것을 끌어올리고 샤워 커튼을 쳤습니다.

커튼이 흔들리고 떨렸습니다.

아서는 비명을 질렀습니다. 그리고 아래층으로 날려 엄마 품속으로 들어갔습니다.

"무슨 일이니?" 그녀가 물었습니다.

아서는 그녀의 팔을 잡고 당겼습니다.

"우리 집 밖으로 가야돼요, 엄마. 그게 너무 커지고 있어요!"

그들이 바깥으로 나오자, 봉투의 한 모서리가 창문 밖으로 꿈틀거리며 움직였습니다. 다른 모서리는 굴뚝 밖으로 튀어나왔습니다.

page 54

"무슨 일이 벌어지고 있는 거야?" 엄마가 물었습니다.

"봉투예요." 아서가 소리 질렀습니다. "그거 열지 마세요! 뭔가 끔찍한 것일 수 있어요!"

그때 집의 지붕이 날아갔습니다. 봉투의 윗면이 떠올랐고, 덮개가 열렸습니다.

D.W.가 튀어나왔습니다.

"나를 속였어, 아서 오빠." 그녀가 말했습니다. "오빠 아직 엄마한테 말하지도 않았어."

"안 돼!" 아서가 울부짖었습니다.

9장

page 55

아서는 일어났습니다. 그의 양손은 얼굴 앞에 겹쳐져 있었습니다.

"이대로 계속할 수는 없어." 그는 중얼거렸습니다. "심지어 서머스쿨도 이것보다는 낫겠어."

그는 아래층으로 걸어갔습니다. 그의 아빠는 여전히 TV를 보고 있었습니다. 그것은 일종의 요리 프로그램이었습니다.

"파슬리, 세이지, 로즈메리 그리고 타임은 좋은 노래 제목이 될 수 있겠지만, 양념으로는 같이 쓰지 마세요."

page 56

"시도할 가치가 있을지도 몰라." 리드 씨가 혼잣말을 했습니다. "아마도 수프에 넣는다든가..."

아서는 계속 갔습니다. 그의 발은 납덩이 같이 느껴졌고, 그의 다리는 슬로우 모션으로 움직이는 것 같았습니다.

봉투는 여전히 휴지통 안에 있었습니다. 아서는 그것을 꺼냈습니다.

그는 엄마의 작업 공간이 있는 다이닝 룸으로 갔습니다.

불이 여전히 켜져 있었습니다.

아서는 심호흡을 했습니다. "이걸 내가 끝낼 때까지 이건 날 계속 괴롭힐 거야."

아서는 다이닝 룸으로 들어갔습니다. "잠깐 1초만 시간 있어요, 엄마?"

엄마가 펜을 내려놓았습니다. "널 위해서는 2초도 있지. 왜 이렇게 늦게까지 일어나 있니?"

page 58

아서는 깊은 숨을 들이쉬었습니다. "그게 내가 엄마하고 이야기해야 하는 것이에요. 저는 집에 오자마자 뭔가를 했어야 했어요. 하지만 제가 사고를 친 것 같아 걱정돼서, 그걸 하지 않았고, 지금은 엄마가 그것 때문에 화를 낼까 봐 두려—"

"진정하렴, 아서! 무슨 일이니? 나한테 말해 봐. 화내지 않을게."

"약속하세요?"

그녀는 끄덕였습니다.

아서는 그녀에게 봉투를 건네줬습니다. 그녀는 그걸 잘라서 열고 안을 들여다봤습니다.

"아! 여기 있었네!" 그녀는 얼굴을 찌푸렸습니다. "아서, 난 밤새 이것을 기다리고 있었어."

아서는 바닥을 바라보았습니다. "저

한테 화내지 않겠다고 약속하셨잖아요."

"그래, 그래, 그랬지." 그의 엄마는 심호흡을 했습니다. "음, 나는 정확히 말하면 화가 난 게 아니야. 당혹스러운 게 더 나은 말인 것 같다. 난 아주 당혹스러워. 나는 몇 시간 동안 허브 씨에게 연락하려고 애썼단다. 나는 이 정보가 필요했어."

page 59

"하지만 이건 하니 교장 선생님한테서 온 건데요."

"(하니는 그의 성이고) 허브가 그의 이름이야."

그녀는 서류를 훑어보았습니다.

"음, 엄마?"

"흠... 응, 아서?"

"그 안에 뭐가 있어요?"

그의 엄마가 올려보았습니다. "세금 서류야. 내가 그의 세금 정산을 한단다."

"저에 관한 건 없어요?"

"네가 하니 교장 선생님이 세금 내는 것을 도와줄 게 아니라면!"

아서는 웃었습니다. "안녕, 서머스쿨." 그는 중얼거렸습니다.

리드 부인은 서류를 잠시 내려놓았습니다. "이제 무슨 일인지 알겠다." 그녀가 말했습니다. "하지만 아서, 만약 이게 너랑 관련된 거였어도, 우리는 무슨 일인지 알 필요가 있어."

page 60

"만약 나쁜 일이었다면요?"

그의 엄마가 한숨 쉬었습니다. "나쁜 소식을 미루는 것이 상황을 좋게 만들지 않아. 때로는 더 나쁘게 만들지. 게다가, 네가 문제를 가지고 있다는 것을 알지 못하면, 아빠와 나는 너를 도와줄 수 없단다."

아서는 끄덕였습니다. "그게 맞는 것 같아요."

"음, 우리 아침에 더 얘기하자. 이제 침대로 돌아가렴. 너무 늦었어."

그녀는 아서에게 키스를 했습니다.

그 모든 걱정이 쓸데없었네, 라고 아서는 생각했습니다. 그는 오후 내내 그리고 저녁까지 아무 이유 없이 스스로를 고문하고 있었습니다.

"힘 내, 아서!" 그의 엄마가 말했습니다. "네가 실망하지 않았길 바란다. 왜냐면 네가 정말 곤경에 빠지길 원한다면, 내가 교장 선생님과 약속을 잡을 수—"

"안녕히 주무세요, 엄마!" 아서는 서둘러 말하고, 문을 향해 뛰어갔습니다.

10장

page 61

아서가 친구들에게 전화하기에는 너

무 늦은 시간이었습니다. 하지만 아서는 그들의 반응이 어떨지 상상할 수 있었습니다.

"너 아직 살아있어?" 프랜신은 말할 것입니다. "잘했어!"

버스터 역시 기뻐할 것입니다. "이제 우리는 여름 내내 같이 지낼 수 있어! 네가 어떤 문제에 빠지든, 내가 바로 옆에 같이 있을게."

"이런." 빙키는 말할 것입니다. "또 곤경에서 벗어났어? 믿을 수가 없네."

아서가 위층으로 올라가려고 하고 있을 때, D.W.가 그를 기다리고 있는 것을 보았습니다.

page 62

"그래서, 나한테 무슨 일이 있었는지 말해 봐!" 그녀가 말했습니다. "1년 동안 외출 금지 당했어? 감옥에 가는 거야? 내가 오빠 방 가져도 돼?"

"침대로 돌아가, 너희 둘!" 엄마가 외쳤습니다.

"저는 그냥 물 마시려고 하는 중이에요." D.W.가 말했습니다. 그녀는 아서를 쳐다보았습니다. "나 대답을 기다리고 있어..."

아서는 어깨를 으쓱했습니다. "실망시켜서 미안, D.W. 하지만 할 말이 없어. 난 네가 어디서 그런 말도 안 되는 생각을 갖게 된 건지 모르겠다."

"말도 안 되는 생각? 어디서 그것을 갖게 됐냐고?" 그녀는 멈춰 생각했습니다. "어디 보자. 공포에 빠져 얼어 있거나, 개구리처럼 안절부절못한 사람은 내가 아니었거든!"

"얼어 있어? 안절부절못해?" 아서의 눈이 활짝 열렸습니다. "대단한 상상력이구나!"

"아 그러지 말고." D.W.가 말했습니다. "말해 봐. 오빠 차고로 이사 가는 거야? 팔이 오빠랑 같이 가? 우리—"

"질문은 이제 됐어." 아서가 말했습니다. "난 너한테 아무것도 말해 주지 않을 거야."

page 64

"안 한다고?"

아서는 미소 지었습니다. "D.W., 이건 네가 스스로 풀어야 할 수수께끼야."

그녀는 그에게 얼굴을 찡그렸지만, 아서는 신경 쓰지 않았습니다. 마침내 그는 기분이 좋아졌습니다.

Chapter 1

1. B Today's choices featured a mystery meat covered in gravy.

2. A They started a game of milk hockey. Francine and Sue Ellen made up one team. Arthur and Buster were the other. They used a crushed milk carton as a puck, hitting it back and forth the length of the table.

3. C *"Attention, please!"* Miss Tingley, the school secretary, was speaking over the loudspeaker. *"Arthur Read, please report to Principal Haney's office immediately."*

4. D "You're in real trouble now, Arthur," said Buster. Sometimes Mr. Haney yelled at him for running through the halls. But he had been to the *office* only once—for putting sneezing powder on Mr. Ratburn's desk.

5. B Arthur slid over his tray. "Help yourself," he said. "I just lost my appetite."

Chapter 2

1. D Arthur let out a sigh. "Mr. Haney gave me this." He held up a large brown envelope. "He said it was for my mom."

2. C Binky folded his arms. "Let's just open." "I can't," said Arthur. "It's addressed to my mother. And look what's stamped on it: PRIVATE and CONFIDENTIAL."

3. B "If it was good news," said Muffy, "Mr. Haney would have told you. My mother always tells me right away if we've gotten a new limousine or if the cook is making a special dessert for dinner." "He didn't say anything like that," Arthur admitted. "That means it's bad news," said Francine. "The question is, how bad is it?"

4. A "All right," said Francine. "But you forced me into it." She shuddered. "What if you didn't pass Mr. Ratburn's history test?"

5. B *He saw himself chained to the wall of a dark dungeon. Outside the barred window, he could hear his friends playing.*

Chapter 3

1. A "Mr. Haney didn't say anything about *when* you should deliver the envelope," the Brain had told him. "Under international law, you have the right to make a plan."

2. C "We have to take action! I don't want to spend all summer doing fun stuff without you." He pushed the envelope toward the edge of the table. "Hey, what if you accidentally lost it?"

3. B "Maybe you could hide it in the laundry basket—and it could get washed." She picked up the envelope and held it carefully as if it were wet and dripping. "She won't be able to read it, but you won't be blamed."

4. B "I don't have that kind of money," said Arthur.

5. A "The whole thing doesn't seem fair," said Arthur. "I didn't do anything! I'll just have to give the envelope to my mother and see what happens."

Chapter 4

1. C "Hello!" Arthur called out softly. No one was in the kitchen except his dog, Pal.

2. A "That's a lot of nothing," said D.W. "You sure are acting weird."

3. A D.W. climbed onto a chair and stared into Arthur's eyes. "You don't fool me," she said. "I know *worry* when I see it." Arthur blinked. "You do?" D.W. nodded. "Yup. You get wrinkles."

4. D "PRIVATE and CONFIDENTIAL." D.W. frowned. "I know PRIVATE. What does CON-FI-DEN-TEE-UL mean." Arthur sighed. "That only Mom can look at it."

5. C D.W.'s eyes opened wide. She got down from the chair and skipped toward the hall, singing, *"Arthur's in trouble, Arthur's in trouble."*

Chapter 5

1. B The good news was that D.W. suddenly stopped singing. The bad news was that she stopped because she had bumped into her mother.

2. A Mrs. Read was an accountant. She always got a little frazzled at tax time.

3. D "Then why did you leave his dish on the table?" She put it down on the floor.

4. B "Mail call!" said Mr. Read, arriving with a bundle of letters. He dropped them on top of Arthur's envelope.

5. D "Talk to you later, Leah." She hung up the phone and dropped the envelope on the edge of the counter. She turned back to the stove. The envelope teetered for a moment—and then fell into the wastebasket.

Chapter 6

1. C Dinner was hard to swallow. How could Arthur concentrate on eating? Every time he looked up, he saw the envelope peeking at him from the wastebasket.

2. B Usually he piled the potato puffs into a castle wall and then lined up the green beans like alligators in the moat.

3. D "Oh, yes. We didn't have all the different projects you kids have today. Sometimes a single test could be half our whole grade." "That much?" His father smiled. "Definitely. I wouldn't say you kids have it easy, but you do have more choices."

4. C "History's important, too," said his father. "I might want to study old recipes or create a meal with some historical theme."

5. A D.W. smiled. "Arthur, isn't there anything else you'd like to give Mom while you're at it?" Arthur just barely kept himself from kicking D.W. under the table. "Just my thanks," he said, "for making this great dinner."

Chapter 7

1. D *Think of a word that rhymes with* rope *and* hope. "Arrghhh!" said Arthur. He switched quickly to math. The first problem involved cutting a rectangle in half. "I wish I could cut that envelope in half," said Arthur. Another question was about a mailbag filled with letters. There was no mention of the *E* word, but that was all Arthur could think about.

2. B *But was it only a rectangle? No, it was a giant envelope, and it was chasing Arthur down a hill.*

3. C "Babies are lucky," he muttered. "They don't have to worry about envelopes. Or history tests. Or summer school. They only have to look cute and fill their diapers."

4. A He found his father and D.W. watching *The Karaoke Kittens* show on TV.

5. D Arthur stood up. If only he could take a pill to get rid of his problem. But things were not that easy.

Chapter 8

1. C As Arthur got ready for bed, he found himself looking at his pillow. He had never noticed before how much it looked like a stuffed envelope. While brushing his teeth, Arthur brought his face right up to the mirror. His teeth lined up in little square rows. Almost like envelopes, he thought. Everywhere he looked—the wallpaper, the carpeting, the pattern on his blanket—he saw envelopes. They came in every shape and size.

2. A Arthur sat up. "What do you want?" "I want to know about the trouble you're in."

3. D Arthur stared at the ceiling. Strictly speaking, he had told D.W. the truth. His mother *hadn't* mentioned to him what was inside the envelope. Of course, that was only because she hadn't *seen* it yet. The envelope was still sitting in the wastebasket.

4. B *Arthur pulled the envelope free and ran upstairs. The envelope was flapping in his arms. It was getting too big to carry. Arthur dragged it along the floor to the bathroom. He hoisted it into the tub and drew the shower curtain.*

5. A *At that moment the roof flew off the house. The top of the envelope rose up, and the flap opened. D.W. popped out. "You tricked me, Arthur," she said. "You haven't even told Mom yet."*

Chapter 9

1. B Arthur woke up. His hands were crossed in front of his face. "I can't go on this way," he muttered. "Even summer school would be better than this."

2. A "Slow down, Arthur! What's going on? You can tell me. I won't get mad."

"Promise?" She nodded.

3. C "What's in there?" His mother looked up. "Tax documents. I'm doing his tax return."

4. B Mrs. Read put down her papers for a moment. "Now I think I understand," she said. "But Arthur, even if this was about you, we would need to know."

5. A "You're not disappointed, I hope. Because if you really want to be in trouble, I'm sure I could arrange—" "Good night, Mom!" Arthur said hurriedly, and bolted for the door.

Chapter 10

1. D It was too late for Arthur to call his friends, but he could imagine their reactions.

2. B Buster would be pleased, too. "Now we'll be together all summer! If you get in any trouble then, I'll be right there beside you."

3. C Arthur shrugged. "Sorry to disappoint you, D.W., but there's nothing to tell. I don't know where you get these crazy ideas." "Crazy ideas? Where do I get them?"

4. D "Are you grounded for a year? Off to jail? Can I have your room?" . . . "Come on," said D.W. "Tell me. Are you moving into the garage? Is Pal moving there with you? Are we—"

5. A Arthur smiled. "D.W., this is one mystery you'll have to solve on your own."